The Romantic Mother

·THE·
R·O·M·A·N·T·I·C
MOTHER

Narcissistic Patterns
in Romantic Poetry

BARBARA A. SCHAPIRO

THE JOHNS HOPKINS UNIVERSITY PRESS
Baltimore and London

The Johns Hopkins University Press, Baltimore, Maryland 21218
The Johns Hopkins Press Ltd., London

Library of Congress Cataloging in Publication Data

Schapiro, Barbara A.
The romantic mother.

Bibliography: p. 137
Includes index.
1. English poetry—19th century—History and
criticism. 2. Romanticism—England. 3. Narcissism
in literature. 4. Mothers in literature. 5. Women
in literature. 6. Psychoanalysis and literature.
I. Title
PR590.S3 1983   821'.7'093520431   82-14023
ISBN 0-8018-2896-1

CONTENTS

I wish to express my sincere gratitude to Rudolf Storch for his advice and guidance throughout my research for this study and to my husband, Scotty, for his continual encouragement and support.

INTRODUCTION

The image of the woman, whether she figures as an ideal goddess or a serpentine vampire, a deserted woman or, more frequently, as the ever-maternal Nature, is central to the poetry of the Romantics. The relationship with the woman which the poetry either expresses or implies is rooted psychologically in the relationship with the first woman of all our lives, the mother. Not only does this relationship occupy a central position in the imagery of every major Romantic poet, but it also bears directly on the particular style and general thematic preoccupations of each. For the psychological dimensions underlying the images of women inform the poetry at its deepest, most fundamental level.

Recent studies on narcissism and on the psychology of the self, particularly those of Heinz Kohut and Otto Kernberg, provide the theoretical framework for my critical analysis. Their writings, as well as those of the British psychologists Melanie Klein, W. D. Fairbairn, Harry Guntrip, and D. W. Winnicott, stress relationships with objects and the formation of an autonomous identity (as opposed to purely sexual drives and impulses) as the crucial factors in psychic development. Their theories all focus on the earliest relationship with the mother as the core experience in one's psychic and emotional maturation. The mother imago, the unconscious representation of the mother, is internalized in infancy and retained throughout adulthood. That unconscious representation is built upon the basis of the first real and fantasized relationship with the mother. Due to the unavoidable shortcomings of maternal care, the relationship with the mother as our first love object is primarily characterized by ambivalence. This ambivalence, as will be explained more fully in the first chapter, is internalized and results in a corresponding split in the ego. The child internalizes both the "good," loving mother and the "bad," frustrating one. If the relation with the mother imago is damaged by such disturbances as separation, death, or emotional rejection, the internal splitting becomes even more intense.

Splitting, as Kernberg explains, is a major cause of ego weakness. Failure to resolve this primitive ambivalence, to integrate the internalized "good" and "bad" objects, prevents both the formation of a mature, cohesive self and the sense of a cohesive, concrete reality outside the self. Such a split internal condition may also result in a regressive desire for refusion with the mother and in a primitive idealization of self and object images. The idealization of the self image compensates for the child's real feelings of deprivation and rage, and the idealization of the parent image compensates for the depriving real parent. These idealizations may combine to form the "grandiose self," and the condition as a whole characterizes pathological narcissism.

Current psychodynamic theories thus describe a deep level of intense, primitive, internalized object relationships. This is useful material for the literary critic, since a work of art, to a large extent, is the manifestation of the emotional dynamics and conflicts of the artist's internal world. Obviously, though, a work of art is more than its psychological roots, and although involvement in emotional conflict may facilitate or bring about creative activity, that activity must ultimately become autonomous and detached from the original conflict, if the artist is to be successful. Such autonomy and detachment, as Ernst Kris explains in *Psychoanalytic Explorations in Art* (1952), is the work of the ego, and the success of a work of art as an aesthetic and social phenomenon is strongly linked to the "intactness of the ego."[1] The creative process always involves a narcissistic regression, what Kris calls "regression in the service of the ego." Thus, the stronger the ego, the greater its capacity to regulate and integrate, the more successful that creative work will be. Ultimately, then, the work of art is not simply an escape into an internal fantasy world but an expression of the struggles and efforts of the ego, of that part of the psyche which is concerned with the individual's relationship with his environment, with reality.

Kris also observes that "the artist whose creative capacities are close to potential pathology will find his place more easily in 'romantic' than in 'classical periods' of art" (p. 30). The works of all the English Romantics indeed display peculiarly strong narcissistic traits. Their poetry in general betrays deeper emotional conflict, more severe disturbances in object relations, and a more vulnerable, exposed ego than do the works of their neoclassical predecessors. The Romantics' feelings of desertion and neglect, of rebellious opposition and revolutionary zeal, are deeply rooted in early emotional experience; at the same time, as Kris argues, historical circumstances always "determine in some way the modes of expression and thus constitute the stuff with which the artist struggles in creation" (p. 15). Romantic poetry gives expression not only to the deep-rooted conflicts in the personality of the poets but also to the essential conflicts dominating the political and social life of their age, the conflicts and upheavals of a society undergoing far-reaching economic and social reforms in the wake of the French Revolution. The Romantics were in conflict with the external, social and material circumstances of their lives, with the parental figures of authority, and such external conflict, as contemporary psychologists are quick to stress, always has an internal reflection.

The seed of English Romanticism, then, is conflict, conflict that has both an internal and an external aspect.[2] The poetry is largely concerned with the subjective experience of the solitary, isolated personality who feels abandoned and deserted as well as angry and rebellious. Although the poetry is characteristically narcissistic, among the works of the various Romantics one can distinguish differences in the levels of narcissistic regression as well as in the strength and intactness of the ego involved. These differences are most evident in the images of women. Some Romantic poets attempt to come to terms with angry and aggressive feelings and allow the woman a concrete, if humanly imperfect, reality, whereas others portray her solely as an abstraction, as split between the ideal maiden and the monstrous witch. The latter poems express the narcissistic wound; the dominant feelings alternate between violent rage and insatiable yearning for total fusion, for death. The self-images in these poems, furthermore, are frequently idealized and grandiose.

Certainly, any psychoanalytic interpretation of literature is open to the danger of reductionism. I believe, however, that an examination of the preoedipal dynamics in Romantic poetry can illuminate underlying dimensions in the structure of the poems and indeed, in some cases, can enable one to see coherence where at first there appears to be none. Also, that the wounded narcissist should be such a characteristic Romantic figure at least suggests that the Romantics were open to the deeper layers of the psyche and in touch with those earliest, formative stages of personality development in which external reality and one's own identity are first being realized. The poetry of the Romantics not only opens and explores new psychic territory but the best of it portrays the struggle of the ego to resolve its internal conflicts and ambivalences, to make contact with reality, and to establish mature object relations.

Of the past criticism on the Romantic movement in general, Mario Praz's *The Romantic Agony* (1933) is perhaps the best-known study of the erotic sensibility of the age. Although Praz was one of the first to discuss the "Romantic" in terms of an "interruption of equilibrium" and to examine the erotic and morbid tendencies in the literature, his study, as he admits himself, is more an exposition and description than it is an analysis. Praz describes, for instance, the pervasive Romantic cult of the Medusa and the joy the Romantics frequently took in the spectacle of tormented beauty. He quotes from Shelley's poem on the picture of the Medusa in the Uffizi Gallery—"'Tis the tempestuous loveliness of terror.'" For the Romantics, Praz notes, Beauty and Death were looked upon as sisters to such an extent that "they became fused into a sort of two-faced herm, filled with corruption and melancholy and fatal in its beauty—a beauty of which, the more bitter the taste, the more abundant the enjoyment" (p. 31). Praz, however, does not analyze or explore the psychic and emotional roots of the condition he describes. His study is a suggestive beginning; by focusing on the image of the Fatal Woman, on the incest theme, and on the influence of the Marquis de Sade in Romantic literature, he opens avenues for psychoanalytic study. Praz's description of the Romantic "Fatal Man," with his "mysterious (but conjectured to be exalted) origin, traces of burnt-out passions, suspicion of a ghastly guilt, melancholy habits, pale face and unforgettable eyes" (p. 59), offers a capsule portrait of the wounded narcissist. By examining the narcissistic personality of this Romantic Fatal Man, one can uncover still deeper relationships and meaning in the poetry. The Fatal Man is intimately bound up with—indeed, is determined by—his relationship with the Romantic Fatal Woman. The fascination (or, more accurately, the obsession) with the Medusa-type woman is more profoundly central to Romantic art than even Praz was aware.

Arthur Wormhoudt's *The Demon Lover: A Psychoanalytic Approach to Literature* focuses on the Romantic's masochistic relationship with the "bad" mother imago. I find Wormhoudt's criticism too mired in clinical terminology to be of much use to the general reader or even to the informed literary critic. Also, several of his interpretations rely on assumptions that are not substantiated by the actual texts. I have the same complaint with Gerald Enscoe's *Eros and the Romantics: Sexual Love as a Theme in Coleridge, Shelley and Keats.* Enscoe's study, moreover, focuses almost exclusively on the psychosexual aspects of the poetry and neglects the many other unconscious fantasies and emotional relationships that the poetry also expresses.

My analysis, which concentrates on two or three representative poems each of Shelley, Keats, Coleridge, and Wordsworth, follows a thematic and developmental, rather than a chronological, order. I consider Shelley's *Alastor* a prototype for the Romantic poem of wounded narcissism. Herbert Read in *The True Voice of Feeling* discusses the essentially narcissistic orientation of Shelley's personality and analyzes the poetry in terms of it. Read believes that Shelley's narcissism is profoundly "healthy" and life-affirming, yet his interpretation is not supported by the poems themselves. In *Alastor,* the ideal maiden whom the Poet seeks throughout the first half of the poem essentially embodies an ideal reflection of the Poet himself. The poem describes a search for the self in intensely erotic terms, and this eroticism is intimately associated with treachery, enervation, and death. Although *Alastor* is a youthful poem, the style and themes are characteristic of Shelley's poetry generally. Even the much later, unfinished *Triumph of Life* reveals the same unresolved ambivalence, the same abstract female and erotic images, that dissolve ultimately into figures of despair and death.

Keats's *Endymion* also portrays the *Alastor* theme of pursuit of an elusive, ideal maiden in an erotic landscape of palaces, streams, and caverns. The poem reveals more of an effort, however, to resist a regressive tendency toward idealization, fusion, and dissolution. Aileen Ward's psychological study, *John Keats: The Making of a Poet*, provides a good basis for my psychoanalytic examination of the poetry. Ward concentrates on Keats's childhood relationship with his mother and on the boy's feelings of betrayal and abandonment at the mother's death. The poetry reveals Keats's unresolved feelings toward the mother image, but these feelings have a source even deeper than the mother's actual death; they are rooted in profound infantile experiences of loss and betrayal. One can, however, observe a progression in Keats's poetry; *The Fall of Hyperion* further chronicles the efforts revealed in *Endymion* to resist a narcissistic regression and to remain in reality.

The relationship with the mother imago in Coleridge's poetry is not only marked by the typical ambivalence but, unlike that in Keats and Shelley, is also colored by feelings of guilt. His poetry displays a greater sense of responsibility for his angry, destructive feelings. Because of the manifest dreamlike, irrational content and the obvious sexual currents, Coleridge's poetry has inspired more psychoanalytic criticism than that of the other Romantics. Beverly Fields in *Reality's Dark Dream: Dejection in Coleridge* as well as Wormhoudt and Enscoe discuss the oedipal and "negative oedipal" patterns in Coleridge's work. J. Garth Ware, Eugene Sloane, and David Beres have also written articles, which I will review in chapter 3, on the ambivalent mother image in the poetry. Virginia Radley in "'Christabel': Directions Old and New" suggests that the ambivalent love relationship is the key to the structure and meaning of *Christabel*. Radley's study, however, remains descriptive, as opposed to psychoanalytic; she suggests a new direction for further critical study. Radley's article is the starting point for my analysis. *Christabel*, I believe, presents the most dramatic example of Coleridge's ambivalent attitude toward the mother imago, and by examining the poem's specific imagery, one can discover both the origins of that attitude in the early narcissistic wound and the guilt and fears of retaliation which accompany it. These psychic and emotional dynamics determine the structure and meaning of the poem at its deepest level. Finally, Coleridge's poetry, as opposed to that of Shelley or Keats, generally does not pursue a regressive desire for refusion with the mother; rather, it expresses an aspiration toward a perfect empathy and communion, toward a balanced, mirroring relationship that does not involve loss of the self. *Frost at Midnight* is his most effective expression of this deeply felt yearning.

Ambivalence and guilt are also the shaping emotions of Wordsworth's poetry. His work, however, records the most strenuous efforts of the self to resolve its split, ambivalent feelings, to externalize, and to integrate itself harmoniously with its environment. Richard Onorato's *The Character of the Poet: Wordsworth in "The Prelude"* offers the most extensive psychoanalytic examination of the poetry. Onorato concentrates on Wordsworth's childhood relationship with his mother and on his feelings of abandonment, grief, and despair at her death. Onorato neglects the deeper infantile ambivalence toward the mother imago and the accompanying feelings of guilt. These feelings, moreover, influence the poetry more profoundly than do the feelings of grief at the mother's actual death.

Several of Wordsworth's early lyrics betray primitive, destructive feelings toward the woman; these feelings, however, are usually halted or checked by the ego and are submitted to the moral demands of the social environment. The emergence of repressed libidinal and aggressive feelings and the halt in the narcissistic regression which occurs at such moments account for the disturbed, uncanny feelings Wordsworth so often records. Although the narcissistic wound is always evident in his poetry, Wordsworth does not succumb to idealized fantasies or to the escapist desire for regressive refusion. His greatest elegies, *Ode: Intimations of Immortality from Recollections of Early Childhood* and *Elegaic Stanzas, Suggested by a Picture of Peele Castle*, detail the psychic movement through loss of original fusion or oneness with the mother to a confrontation with intensely ambivalent feelings and finally to an acceptance of aloneness and a reconciliation with reality. The psychic maturation that the elegies chronicle is reflected in the one most characteristic female image in the poetry—the suffering and forsaken woman.

The image of the abandoned woman, isolated in a hostile environment, reflects the poet's angry destructive feelings as well as his resolution of those feelings. Although the women are still the objects of his deep rage, Wordsworth allows them their wholeness and humanity; his women suffer and endure; their love, their "goodness" survives. Margaret, of *The Ruined Cottage*, for instance, is portrayed concretely and compassionately. The abandoned women reveal the poet's ability to keep the "good" mother imago intact despite the violence of the infantile rage and aggression directed toward it. The poetry continually portrays Wordsworth's confrontation with enraged, destructive feelings and his efforts to keep the woman whole. The greatest moments in his poetry express that achievement; they celebrate a liberation, a real resolution, of the unconscious ambivalent love relationship at the core of the personality.

·1·
SHELLEY

ALASTOR: THE QUEST
OF THE WOUNDED NARCISSIST

Introduction

In a note published with *Alastor*, Mary Shelley remarks, "None of Shelley's poems is more characteristic than this." The plight of an alienated, lone Poet wandering through Nature's labyrinths in search of an elusive, ideal maiden is a distinctive Shelleyan theme. Yet the meaning of this central theme and the coherence of the poem have greatly troubled critics, and *Alastor* has provoked more controversy than any of Shelley's other poems. Raymond Havens began the debate by complaining that the poetry is not consistent with the preface,[1] which asserts that the poem is an allegory: a youth, no longer content with the familiar objects of the world, "thirsts for intercourse with an intelligence similar to itself. He images to himself the Being whom he loves. . . . He seeks in vain for a prototype of his conception. Blasted by his disappointment, he descends to an untimely grave." Shelley then moralizes, "The picture is not barren of instruction to actual men. The Poet's self-centered seclusion was avenged by the furies of an irresistible passion pursuing him to speedy ruin."

Havens argues, however, that in the narrative the Poet does not spend his time seeking for "a prototype of his conception" but in "trying to stifle the pain of separation and in deciding whether or not death may be the doorway to reunion." Havens cannot reconcile the proclaimed moral lesson with the deliberate, indeed ecstatic, movement toward death, nor with the portrait of the Poet as "Gentle and brave and generous," and as a victim of a "fair friend," of a spirit that is seemingly both loving and evil. Finally, Havens complains that the verse itself lacks unity, that there are unnecessary, gratuitous passages—"pictures of nature for their own sake." In reply to Havens, critics have established the poem's meaning and coherency by offering a variety of autobiographical and allegorical readings.[2] I have found no analysis, however, which in any way elucidates the connection between the Poet's idealism and the erotic and suicidal themes that troubled Havens, nor any adequate explanation for the discrepant pictures of nature and their function in the poem. An examination of the poem from a psychological perspective, however, casts some light on these questions. Viewed psychologically, the poem's apparent incoherence becomes a meaningful expression of a personality that lacks a solid coherent identity. At the core of this unstable identity or self is a highly ambivalent relationship with the mother imago. An examination of the female figures in *Alastor* reveals this central ambivalent relationship.

The Women

Women figure in *Alastor* in three essential forms: the ideal, visionary maiden; weeping virgins who shower the Poet with love and pity; and Nature, whom the Poet addresses as "Mother of this unfathomable world." Whereas the loving virgins are a simple fantasy, the ideal maiden and the images of nature are psychologically more complex. The purpose of the lengthy nature descriptions indeed puzzled Havens. Yet from the beginning, the poem establishes the maternal image of Nature as both fundamental and integral to the overall themes of alienation and quest. *Alastor* opens with a direct address to the Mother in which the poet avows his love and anxiously appeals for her favor. After first asking the "Earth, ocean, air" to "forgive this boast," he proceeds: "Mother of this unfathomable world! / Favour my solemn song, for I have loved / Thee ever, and thee only" (18-20). Immediately the mother image is associated with shadows, darkness, mystery, and death:

> . . . I have watched
> Thy shadow, and the darkness of thy steps,
> And my heart ever gazes on the depth
> Of thy deep mysteries. I have made my bed
> In charnels and on coffins, where black death
> Keeps record of the trophies won from thee,
> Hoping to still these obstinate questionings
> Of thee and thine, by forcing some lone ghost
> Thy messenger, to render up the tale
> Of what we are.
>
> [21-29]

The mother witholds her secrets, her love—"ne'er yet / Thou hast unveiled thy inmost sanctuary," Shelley says several lines later. She is indeed intimately related to the poet's expressed feelings of unreality and lack of identity. It is only from the "lone ghost" and among the oft-mentioned "twilight phantasms" that the poet gropes for the answer to "what we are."

Nature is thus as mysterious and elusive as the visionary ideal maiden. The Poet must pursue "Nature's most secret steps . . . like her shadow" (81-82). As he then makes his solitary pursuit, the most remarkable feature of the natural landscape which emerges is its alternating appearance as either desolate and destructive or enveloping and voluptuous. He roams, for instance, where

> The red volcano overcanopies
> Its fields of snow and pinnacles of ice
> With burning smoke, or where bitumen lakes
> On black bare pointed islets ever beat
> With sluggish surge, . . .
>
> [83-87]

Even the enveloping bowers, however, the soft, leafy dells and "embosoming vales" are potentially menacing and destructive. With their "clasping ivy," "entwining arms," "clenching" and "grasping roots," they threaten an annihilating suffocation. Nature, or the Mother, is thus conceived as both barren and overwhelming. The landscape is a familiar one in Shelley's poetry. Images of "icy caverns" and "desolate shores," of "embosoming dells" and "vaulted bowers," figure in *The Revolt of Islam, Epipsychidion*, and *Prometheus Unbound*, among others. The involved, shifting

pictures of nature in *Alastor*, for which Havens could find no
reason, thus actually compose a psychic landscape that is central
to this as well as to many other Shelleyan poems. Nature is portrayed as not only mysterious and elusive but inconstant and
treacherous—even her womb-like dells and havens ultimately lead
to death. The ambivalence that she inspires is the crucial tension
on which the poem works.

Shelley also exposes this ambivalent attitude in a short lyric
published with *Alastor*. The untitled verse is addressed to Coleridge, who, Shelley says, has "turned from men" to commune with
the spirits of Nature:

> With mountain winds, and babbling springs,
>   And moonlight seas, that are the voice
> Of these inexplicable things,
>   Thou didst hold commune, and rejoice
> When they did answer thee; but they
> Cast, like a worthless boon, thy love away.
>
> Ah! wherefore didst thou build thine hope
>   On the false earth's inconstancy?
> Did thine own mind afford no scope
>   Of love, or moving thoughts to thee?
> That natural scenes or human smiles
> Could steal the power to wind thee in their wiles?
>
> [6-25]

This interpretation of Coleridge's crisis, as Harold Bloom points
out in *The Visionary Company*, is actually contrary to Coleridge's
own understanding of Nature in which "we receive but what we
give / And in our life alone does Nature live." Shelley's Nature has
a life apart from our own but, as Bloom observes, she "is necessarily false and inconstant to us. Or, to put it as a contrary of
Wordsworth's language, Nature always will and must betray the
human heart that loves her, for Nature . . . is not adequate to meet
the demands made upon her by the human imagination. So, from
the beginning, Shelley takes his position with Blake as against
Wordsworth."[3] Although I agree with the alliance between Shelley
and Blake, I am uncomfortable with Bloom's summation of their
relationship with Nature. If the love of woman and the love of
Nature are, as Bloom later acknowledges, directly associated, then

what is the meaning and what are the consequences of Blake and Shelley's attitude? To explain that the poets reject Nature/woman because she stifles the imagination does not settle the troublesome fact that they are rejecting reality for solitary narcissistic fantasy. Shelley's intensely subjective, abstract style, the organization of his poems around infantile fantasies of persecution and betrayal, the primitive images of a grandiose self that is yet at bottom an empty, fragmented self, are all rooted in his profound and unresolved ambivalence toward the mother. This ambivalence indeed extends toward women in general. Although I will provide a more detailed psychological explanation later, at the moment I simply wish to point out the close connection between this ambivalence and the theme of a lost and unformed self which the poetry itself reveals. The portrait of the ideal maiden in *Alastor* further illustrates this connection.

The Poet first experiences the vision of his ideal mate while ensconced in a womblike dell "where odorous plants entwine /Beneath the hollow rocks a natural bower."

> . . . A vision on his sleep
> There came, a dream of hopes that never yet
> Had flushed his cheek. He dreamed a veiled maid
> Sate near him, talking in low solemn tones.
> Her voice was like the voice of his own soul
> Heard in the calm of thought; . . .
>
> [149-54]

The most significant point about the maiden is that her voice "Was like the voice of his own soul." She is the ideal image or reflection of the Poet himself. She is indeed "herself a poet" (161). This fantasy of an ideal woman which is intimately tied to the fantasy of an ideal self again forms a familiar motif in Shelley's poetry. Laon in *The Revolt of Islam* describes Cythna "As mine own shadow . . . A second self" (874-75), and Cythna later in disguise calls herself "Laone." The incestuous basis of their relationship is also apparent; Cythna, an orphan, was raised by Laon's parents and the two grew up as brother and sister. An incestuous passion for one's sister, as Freud has shown, is rooted in the illicit sensual feelings originally experienced in relation to the mother. Thus, at the root of Laon's love for his sister/ideal self is again the ambivalent mother imago.

The poet's love for Emily in *Epipsychidion* is also revealed as a
love of self:

> Would we two had been twins of the same mother!
> Or, that the name, my heart lent to another
> Could be a sister's bond for her and thee,
> Blending two beams of one eternity!
> . . . .
> How beyond refuge I am thine. Ah me!
> I am not thine: I am part of *thee.*
>
> [45-52]

This fantasized love of an ideal maiden/self, however, is inevitably
doomed to dissolution and failure. The scenes of erotic union in
Shelley's poetry are almost always scenes of death. The following
passage from *Alastor* is typical:

> His strong heart sunk and sickened with excess
> Of love. He reared his shuddering limbs and quelled
> His gasping breath, ...
> With frantic gesture and short breathless cry
> Folded his frame in her dissolving arms.
> Now blackness veiled his dizzy eyes, and night
> Involved and swallowed up the vision; sleep,
> Like a dark flood suspended in its course,
> Rolled back its impulse on his vacant brain.
>
> [181-89]

Eroticism is continually associated with sickness, enervation,
and dissipation. When Laon reunites with Cythna in *The Revolt
of Islam*, for instance, he experiences "the sickness of a deep / And
speechless swoon of joy" (2636-37), and the ecstasy that the poet
in *Epipsychidion* experiences while describing the moment of fusion with Emily does not hide the equally intense feelings of dissolution and despair:

> We shall become the same, we shall be one
> Spirit within two frames, oh! wherefore two?
> One passion in twin hearts, ...
> One Heaven, one Hell, one immortality,
> And one annihilation. Woe is me!
> The winged words on which my soul would pierce

Into the height of Love's rare Universe,
Are chains of lead around its flight of fire—
I pant, I sink, I tremble, I expire!

[572-98]

Thus, as Nature is ambivalently conceived, so is the ideal maiden, so indeed are all the female images in Shelley's poetry. Just as Nature is portrayed as inconstant and untrustworthy, so Shelley's favorite adjective for the maiden is "treacherous." Not only is her disappearance felt to be an abandonment and betrayal but her love leads only to death. The ambivalent feelings lurking in the love for the ideal maiden are most pronounced in *Epipsychidion* where, at one point, the forlorn poet sees a "fair form" resembling the vanished Emily and describes her voice as "venomed melody," her touch as "electric poison," and her cheeks and bosom as sending forth "a killing air" (259-61). Yet these ambivalently conceived women always seem to hold the key to the Poet's identity. Nature's "inmost sanctuary" is secret, witheld, and veiled, but holds the answer, the Poet believes, to "what we are." The visionary maiden is also inextricably connected to the Poet's sense of identity: she is indeed imaged as his ideal or second self. Shelley's poetry thus raises several questions: Why is the woman portrayed so ambivalently? Why does she hold the key to the Poet's identity? Why is eroticism associated with sickness and death and a love union inevitably doomed? Contemporary theories on the psychology of the self, and on narcissism in particular, have addressed themselves to such questions and thus they can offer a vocabulary for further analysis.

Narcissism: A Review of Clinical Theory and Its Application to Romantic Poetry

Although many critics have noted the narcissistic element in Shelley's poetry, only Sir Herbert Read, to my knowledge, has commented on it extensively as a means of illuminating the poetry.[4] His analysis, however, is extremely misleading. Read relies less on Freud than on Trigant Burrow, whose "principle of primary identification" Read sees as the key to understanding Shelley's poetry. Primary identification, similar to Freud's concept of primary narcissism, is the "subjective undifferentiated phase of consciousness tending always towards closer consolidation of the mother with itself." This "organic mental bond" or "subjective unity" with the mother, if maintained, leads naturally to autoeroticism and homosexuality for the mother's love object becomes one's own. One's own body, in other words, becomes the love object. Shelley, Read explains, "belonged to a definite psychological type—a type whose consciousness is incompletely objectified, which is therefore evidently narcissistic and unconsciously homosexual." Read defends this neurotic position, however, because he claims that "social adaptation is a compromise," and that by refusing to compromise, Shelley is actually nearer the source of life, closer to "the organic reality." Shelley, he concludes, "was a genius whose neurotic reaction, for all its distortion, represents an organic urge towards a completer oneness of life and a clearer, more conscious social order" (p. 263).

Not only does Read's interpretation fall apart in the light of current psychological theory but, more importantly, in the light of Shelley's poetry itself, which the critic failed to examine carefully enough. Why, for instance, do those scenes in Shelley's poetry of erotic fusion and "organic unity" (which Read claims are "healthy" outside a societal context) always dissolve into images of desolation and death? Why do the images of Nature/Mother (the source of that joyous organic oneness) so often project feelings of treachery and devastation? And how can a regressive fusion or oneness, which the poetry repeatedly shows to be both morbid and impossible, lead to any serious social order? Much of Shelley's poetry, and *Alastor* in particular, describes a schizoid-narcissistic condition that is incapable of leading to any realistic social or moral order. As a result, the poems frequently collapse into self-pity, desolation, and despair. Matthew Arnold indeed concluded his essay on Shelley with the claim, "The man Shelley, in very truth, is not entirely sane, and Shelley's poetry is not entirely sane either." A brief examination of the theory of narcissism as found in Freud and in post-Freudian theories of object relations sheds light on the schizoid-narcissistic orientation of Shelley's poetry.

In his 1914 article "On Narcissism: An Introduction" Freud states: "The libido withdrawn from the outer world has been directed on to the ego, giving rise to a state which we may call narcissism" (p. 32). Such withdrawal and redirection of the libido, he goes on to describe, leads to an overestimation of the power of wishes and mental processes, the omnipotence of thoughts, and a belief in the magical virtue of words. The transference of libidinal cathexis, which characterizes narcissism, can be observed, Freud says, in the phenomena of organic disease, hypochondria, and love between the sexes. If someone is suffering organic pain, he "relinquishes his interest in the things of the outside world" and "withdraws libidinal interest from his love objects" (p. 39). The same is true in the case of the hypochondriac, although the source of the organic problem lies in an original redirection of libidinal cathexis. In a later article on schizophrenia (1922), Freud also speaks of the "withdrawal of libido from objects and its introduction into the ego." He explains that "the clamorous symptoms of the disease arise from the vain struggles of the libido to find its way back to the objects."[5]

In examining the behavior of human beings in love, Freud first postulates a primary narcissism in everyone. Before the infant has differentiated itself from its mother, its "first auto-erotic sexual gratifications are experienced in connection to self-preservation" (p. 44). All libido originally lies in the ego (or id, as the ego has not yet clearly been differentiated)—"the sexual instincts are at the outset supported upon the ego-instincts" (p. 44). Freud claims that this primary narcissism "may in the long run manifest itself as dominating his object choice" (p. 45). A human being originally has two sexual objects to choose from—the mother and the self. Freud calls the first "anaclitic" love, or object love. The anaclitic type may love the woman who tends or the man who protects. The second choice, in which one chooses oneself or a similar person as the sexual object, Freud terms "narcissistic" object choice. Narcissistic types may love not only their actual selves but also what they once were, or what they would like to be, or even "someone who was once part of" themselves (p. 47). The remainder of Freud's article is concerned with the concept of the "ego-ideal," which he claims is a form of repression and sublimation of the lost gratifications of early narcissism. The self-love that the real ego enjoyed in childhood narcissism is displaced onto the new ideal ego. Freud explains that if one is "not willing to forgo his narcissistic perfection in his childhood, and if, as he develops, he is disturbed by the admonitions of others and his own critical judgement is awakened, he seeks to recover the early perfection, thus wrested from him, in the form of an ego-ideal" (p. 51).

Thus, the essential principle behind Freud's theory of narcissism is the withdrawal of libido from external, actual objects and onto the ego or the imaginary ego ideal. Although the theory is grounded, as always in Freud, in the sexual instincts, specifically in autoerotic gratification, it also looks forward to post-Freudian theories of object relations. Michael Balint in "Primary Narcissism and Primary Love" (1960) proposes doing away with the notion of primary narcissism altogether. Instead, he wishes to speak only of primary love. He complains that Freud's terms—primary autoeroticism, primary object love, and primary narcissism—all overlap and contradict one another. In explaining his concept of primary love, Balint refers to the first "harmonious mix-up" in the fetal stage. The individual, he says, is born in a state of intense relatedness to the environment, both biologically and libidinally, and "the aim of all human strivings is to establish—or, probably, re-establish an all-embracing harmony with one's environment, to be able to love in peace." He goes on to explain that whenever a developing relationship to a part of the environment or to an object is in painful contrast to the earlier undisturbed harmony, libido may be withdrawn into the ego in an attempt to regain the previous feeling of oneness. All narcissism, he says, is secondary to the original mix-up and is caused by a disturbance between the individual and the environment.

Balint's theory of narcissism still shares with Freud's, however, the central idea of the redirection of the libido from the external to the internal, from the object to the ego. The concept, so crucial to later theories of object relations, finds further elaboration in Freud's "Mourning and Melancholia" (1917). The melancholic reaction to a lost or abandoned love object, according to Freud, is determined by the internalization of that abandoned object and the identification of the ego with it. The loss of the object is transformed into loss in the ego, and any former conflict between the ego and the loved person is transformed into a cleavage in the ego itself. Ambivalence in the love relations with the lost object leads to a sense of guilt, to a feeling of blame for the death due to the buried hostile, aggressive feelings. Such feelings, Freud claims, may result in suicidal urges and sadism directed at oneself; the hostility formerly directed toward the loved one is now directed onto the self. In intense love and suicide, Freud says, the ego is overwhelmed by the internalized object. Certainly the pervasive Romantic melancholia, as well as tendencies, particularly in Shelley's poetry, toward both ecstatic worship of an ideal love object and enraged sadism and masochism, are illuminated by Freud's discussion. His theory of melancholia, with its emphasis on the processes of internalization and identification following loss of a loved object, and on the resulting ego split due to ambivalence, provides the roots for contemporary theories of object relations.

"A psychodynamic theory is now emerging," writes Harry Guntrip, "which takes into account the fact that man lives in two worlds at the same time, inner and outer, psychic and material, and has relationships with two kinds of objects—internal and external."[6] As opposed to a psychology of drives and impulses, post-Freudian theories stress relationships with objects and identify the underlying psychic problem as that of identity. "The significance of human living lies in object-relationships, and only in such terms can life be said to have a meaning, for without object-relations the ego itself cannot develop," Guntrip states.[7] The relationship with the mother as the first love object not only sets the stage for all later social relations but establishes the very foundation of one's identity and of one's ability to perceive external reality. Guntrip explains that only a whole self, an identity, can recognize the not-self and relate to a real world. Similarly, after an extensive study of infants in their first months of life, Rene Spitz claims that "by far the most important factor in enabling the child to build gradually a coherent ideational image of his world derives from the reciprocity between mother and child."[8]

Melanie Klein's pioneering work in the field of early mother-child relations established the groundwork for object relations psychology. Klein postulates two essential stages, or "positions," in the developing infant-mother relationship. The first stage she calls the "schizoid-narcissistic position," in which the primary mode of relationship is oral—that of infant to mother's breast. According to Klein, this earliest experience at the mother's breast is an essential determinant of an individual's sexual and emotional health. If the experience is a frustrating or ungratifying one, it will arouse intense feelings of hostility, fear, and despair. At this stage of development, the mother is not yet perceived as a whole being apart from the infant's needs; she is simply split as "good" (the source of libidinal gratification) and "bad" (as she frustrates or deprives libidinal needs). And because the bad mother is intolerably threatening, the baby internalizes this bad mother in an attempt to make her good symbolically.[9]

As no mother could possibly satisfy all of an infant's needs all of the time, every mother is inevitably experienced as both good and bad. The more frustrating, or bad, the mother is, however, the more terrifying and persecutory the inner psychic world of the child will be due to the terrifyingly bad internal object. The bad, depriving mother also intensifies the infant's needs to the extent that the neediness itself becomes threatening. The baby feels so "hungry" it fears it will completely devour its object, good as well as bad, thus destroying what it loves. This intense hunger so determines the baby's experience that it also projects it onto its mother and dreads that she will devour it. The schizoid-narcissistic stage is thus characterized by a deep ambivalence, a "love made hungry,"—a terror of annihilation and an overall feeling of futility and emptiness.

The second stage of development, according to Klein, involves the realistic acceptance of the mother as a whole person, both good and bad, as apart from and other than the self. As the me and not-me are now distinguished, the me can feel concern for the possible effect of its anger (due to frustration at lack of love) on the not-me. Klein thus calls this stage the "depressive position." The fear is no longer that one's love will destroy but that one's hate will destroy, and these destructive, hateful feelings give rise to a severe sense of guilt. As D. W. Winnicott explains, "Guilt is related to the idea of destruction where love is also operating." Winnicott calls this depressive position "the stage of concern" and explains that the social impulses begin here. "Being depressed," he claims, "is an achievement, and implies a high degree of personal integration, and an acceptance of responsibility for all the destructiveness that is bound up with living, with the instinctual life, and with anger at frustration."[10] Thus, the integration of love and hatred is, paradoxically, a prerequisite for the capacity to experience normal love. The ability to suffer guilt and depression, in other words, marks the first movement out of narcissistic isolation and into mature object relations.

Finally, the two leading theories on narcissism today, those of Heinz Kohut and Otto Kernberg, are also firmly based in object relations psychology. Although Kohut rejects most of Klein's particular theories, he still builds his psychology of the self on the dynamics of the early mother-child relationship. Because the mother is initially so closely and libidinally tied to the child, is indeed experienced as part of the child's self, Kohut refers to her as a "self-object." In *The Analysis of the Self* he explains that narcissism is founded in a relationship with objects "used in the service of the self" or with objects "experienced as part of the self." He retains Freud's notion of primary narcissism and claims that this primary narcissism is always disturbed by the unavoidable short-comings of maternal care. The child thus compensates by estab-lishing either a grandiose and exhibitionistic image of the self—the "grandiose self"—or an idealized parent image—an "omnipotent self-object." This occurs, Kohut believes, in all individuals, and narcissism, the libidinal investment in the self, forms a normal stage in the healthy development of a personality. The narcissistic personality, however, is characterized by a regressive fixation on either the archaic, grandiose self-configurations or the archaic, overestimated, narcissistically cathectic objects (parent imagos).

From the beginning, Kohut argues, the child asserts its need for a food-giving and "appropriately responding" self-object. Appro-priate response includes not only the actual feeding but also what Kohut calls "mirroring"—allowing the child to feel acknowledged, approved of, loved. The child, he believes, must also be allowed to idealize the self-object and to feel an "empathetic merger" with it. These self/self-object relations, he maintains, are the precursors of psychic structures, and in normal development the internalization of the self-objects leads gradually to the consolidation of the self.

Otto Kernberg in *Borderline Conditions and Pathological Nar-cissism* differs from Kohut in his belief that pathological narcis-sism is not simply a fixation on a normal primitive self but on a pathological self-structure. This pathological structure, he argues, is different from infantile narcissism and, in fact, prohibits the healthy, normal libidinal investment of the self. The premise of Kernberg's argument is that narcissistic investment and object in-vestment occur simultaneously and so intimately influence one another that one cannot be studied without the other. Objects are originally introjected, he explains, under two drive derivatives—li-bidinal and aggressive. The child internalizes both good, loved objects and bad, hated ones. This division is first due to the lack of integrative capacity of the early ego. Later, however, this lack of integrative capacity can be used defensively by the emerging ego in order to prevent generalization of anxiety and to protect the ego core built around the positive introjections (the good objects). There are two essential tasks, Kernberg explains, that the early ego must accomplish: differentiation of self-images from object images and integration of libidinally and aggressively determined self-images and object images.

Excessive frustration in the earliest stages, however, may result in either a disposition toward regressive refusion or an intensification and fixation on the splitting process. Splitting is the fundamental cause of ego weakness and occurs in combination with "primitive idealization." The idealization of self-images and object images both acts as a protection against the surrounding world of bad, persecuting, and dangerous objects and contains a hopeless yearning and love for an ideal mother. The idealization is both defensive and compensatory; the fantasy of an ideal, omnipotent self compensates for severe oral frustration, rage, and envy, and the fantasy of an ever-giving, ever-loving, accepting parent compensates for the depriving realistic one. The ideal self-images and ideal object images combine, Kernberg says, to form the "grandiose self." Besides resulting in the idealization, however, splitting also leads to the projection or externalization of all-bad, aggressive self-images and object images. There is a general devaluation of the external world, and the inner world of the narcissistic personality consists of idealized representations of the self, "shadows" of others, and dreaded enemies. The deepest image of the narcissist's relationship with external objects is that of a "hungry, enraged, empty self, full of impotent anger at being frustrated and fearful of a world as hateful and revengeful as the patient himself" (p. 233).

In conclusion, one of the most important aspects of object relations theory as it relates to Romantic poetry is the fundamental connection it posits between one's earliest human love relationships, one's sense of identity, and one's ability to perceive and accept painful reality. As Arnold Modell explains, learning and loving are highly interrelated, and "the ego structure whose development permits the acceptance of painful reality is identical to that structure whose development enables one to love maturely."[11] The premise behind this thesis is that for the young child, the mother and the environment are synonymous, or, as Spitz explains it, "In the mother-child relation the mother represents the environmental givens—or one might say that the mother *is* the representative of the environment."[12]

The relationship with this earliest environment is essentially ambivalent, much as Freud has shown in *Totem and Taboo* that primitive man's relationship with the environment is basically ambivalent — the environment provides the cycle of both death and creation. This leads Modell to propose an analogy between the historical development of society's acceptance of an inanimate world and the process in the individual that permits the acceptance of "reality." Magical thinking, Modell says, is the primitive mode of relationship to the environment, characterized by omnipotent fantasies and by a denial of separateness between the self and the environment. The structure of magical thought itself, however, is ambivalent; the self and/or the environment may be experienced as possessing an omnipotent force of both limitless good and unlimited destruction. In normal development, however, the ego becomes well-integrated and autonomous enough to allow for the separateness of objects and to accept the painful reality that they can be lost.

Shelley's poetry, as well as much of Blake's, exemplifies the primitive, fractured vision of the narcissist who is trapped within a private, ambivalently determined, magical world of angels and demons and who is unable to make contact with any concrete external reality. Their poetry abounds in images of splitting and fusing, of hungry, devouring figures, and in images of an idealized, grandiose self in an abstracted world of hostile, tyrannous figures. A severely split ego, as Kernberg explains, is unable to integrate the good and bad objects into a single separate reality, to achieve Klein's depressive position. It is unable to mourn over its good lost objects and to feel regret and guilt over its aggression. Kernberg also discusses how the bad internal objects, the sadistic forerunners of the superego, can distort the perception of parental images and prevent the integration of a normal superego. Instead, there results a lack of realistic differentiation between mother/father and a consequent combined dangerous mother/father image. All sexual relationships are later conceived as dangerous and aggressively infiltrated. Again, the poetry of Shelley, and much of Blake, portrays sexual relationships as treacherous and devastating with hermaphroditic creatures figuring in the works of both. In the emotional landscape of Shelley's poetry, furthermore, guilt is conspicuously absent. His work is swept instead by schizoid-narcissistic feelings

of impotent rage and persecution, by self-pity, and by an overall sense of futility and despair.

Thus, another look at *Alastor* reveals that the poem indeed assumes a definite coherence—the coherence albeit of a personality that lacks a cohesive, integrated self. The subjective, abstract style, the themes of loss, alienation, and futile idealistic quest, the ambivalent images of saving/treacherous women, the confluence of eroticism and death, and the atmosphere of unreality and emptiness are all one; together they constitute the lament of a wounded narcissist who has never been able to resolve the intense ambivalence of his earliest love relationship.

A Summary Reading

Alastor opens, as mentioned previously, with an address to the "Mother of this unfathomable world." The passage imagistically associates the mother with mystery and death and with the poet's feelings of unreality and lack of identity. The poem then launches into the story of the lonely, wandering Poet. Immediately, the narcissistic wound and the feeling of self-pity are exposed:

> There was a Poet whose untimely tomb
> No human hands with pious reverence reared,
> . . . .
> He lived, he died, he sung in solitude.
> . . . .
>   When early youth had passed, he left
> His cold fireside and alienated home
> To seek strange truths in undiscovered lands.
>   [50-51, 60, 75-77]

The Poet is like the phantom figure who comes to mourn in *Adonais*, a "frail form" who is "the last, neglected and apart," with a branded brow "like Cain or Christ." He is like the "blighted plant" of *The Zucca* which the Earth has "crushed" on her "unmaternal breast." The figure perhaps first appears in the prose romance *Zastrozzi*, which Shelley wrote while still a schoolboy at Eton. He describes the young hero, Verezzi, as having been "torn from the society of all he held dear on earth, the victim of secret enemies, and exiled from happiness."[13] Most of Shelley's central figures feel betrayed, abandoned, victimized. This is equally true

of Byron's characters, although with one crucial difference: Byron's people usually feel in some sense responsible for their condition and are thus less tormented by others than by their own sense of guilt. Conrad, in *The Corsair*, for instance, believes he was "by Nature sent / To lead the guilty" for he "knew himself a villain." Byron's romances, excepting the satiric *Don Juan*, all tell of an ideal consuming love that leads to acts of treachery and destruction.[14] It is less the woman's love that taints and destroys, however, than the hero's own. Childe Harolde cries that his "kiss had been pollution," and Manfred, that "my embrace was fatal." Manfred's description of his beloved Astarte is indeed strikingly similar to the *Alastor* Poet's vision of his ideal mate/self:

> She was like me in lineaments; her eyes,
> Her hair, her features, all, to the very tone
> Even of her voice, they said were like to mine;
> But soften'd all, and temper'd into beauty:
> She had the same lone thoughts and wanderings,
> The quest of hidden knowledge, and a mind
> To comprehend the universe: . . .
>
> [105-10]

Unlike Shelley's Poet, however, Manfred exclaims, "I loved her and destroyed her!" Shelley's poetry never locates the source of hostility and aggression in the self, and thus his poems most frequently conclude with a self-pitying lament, a cry of victimization, or with a grandiose fantasy of secret power and with a denial of death and destruction. In *The Revolt of Islam*, for instance, both Laon and Laone exert a "secret strength," a "secret power" that, typically, is their power of speech, their poetic eloquence. At the end of the poem, Laon goes smiling to the stake, secretly exulting in his superior martyrdom. The final vision is a paradisiacal image of Laon and Laone soaring off in a winged boat to the Temple of the Spirit. The womblike winged boat that allows the hero to escape the tumult and pains of earthly reality, and most importantly, the reality of death, is one of Shelley's favorite images. *Prometheus Unbound* ends with a similar ascent, a similar escape into a protective, encompassing spirit world of "spheres within spheres" and "orbs involving and involved." In *The Sensitive Plant*, another fantasy about a frail and victimized yet secretly superior self, Shelley again denies the reality of death. As Rudolf Storch has pointed out, "the allegorical projection of the poet's self into the natural object is unmistakable." Storch's interpretation of the poem emphasizes its narcissistic character. The plant is "the feeblest and yet the favorite" of the maternal figure who tends to the garden. When the lady dies, the sensitive plant withers. As Storch observes,

> Shelley then evades the fact of mortality by abstracting it from common life. In the "Conclusion" he argues that since everything in life is deceptive and we are shadows of a dream, we may assume that death itself is an illusion.

> > That garden sweet, that lady fair,
> > And all sweet shapes and odours there,
> > In truth have never passed away;
> > 'Tis we, 'tis ours, are changed; not they.

> > For love, and beauty, and delight,
> > There is no death nor change; their might
> > Exceeds our organs, which endure
> > No light, being themselves obscure.

> In the end we are left with the feeling that the plant and the guardian lady are identified with each other: they die together and also gain immortality together. By denying the mortality of the maternal lady, the sensitive plant, too, seems assured of eternal life.[15]

The solitary, sensitive, unloved Poet of *Alastor* is thus a familiar Shelleyan figure. Cast aloft on that "little boat," the Poet safely has fled a storm, Shelley says, "As if that frail and wasted human form, / Had been an elemental god" (350-51). Feeling both victimized and secretly superior, the Poet is a wandering Narcissus. At one point he actually comes upon some narcissus flowers and longs "To deck with their bright hues his withered hair." As he pursues his solitary journey, the natural landscape, as noted before, is pictured as either frozen and barren or voluptuous and overwhelming. Nature, or the Mother, offers no love, no affirmation of the Poet's being or identity. Wandering among some "awful ruins" he lingers among the temples where "dead men / Hang their mute thoughts on the mute walls around" (120). Or again, he cries of "wasting these surpassing powers / In the deaf air, to the blind earth, and heaven / That echoes not my thoughts" (290). The image is of Narcissus without an echo. Like the infant unloved and unacknowledged by his mother, the Poet feels empty and unreal because unrealized by his environment.

The infantile fears and enraged self-pity give way around line 120, however, to infantile wish-fulfillment fantasies. The Poet describes an Arab maiden who steals away from her father's tent to tend to him and bring him food, though "not daring for deep awe / To speak her love" (1345). Such maidens, who shower him with love and pity, appear occasionally in the poem: "virgins, as unknown he passed, have pined / And wasted for fond love of his wild eyes" (62-64), or "youthful maidens . . . would press his pallid hand / At parting, and watch, dim through tears, the path / Of his departure . . ." (266-71). Immediately following the description of the Arab maiden, however, the most crucial fantasy of the poem, the vision of the ideal maiden, occurs. I have already mentioned the most important point about this maiden—she reflects an ideal image of the Poet himself. Klein believes that the fantasy of having a twin is psychologically bound up with a longing to be understood by the internalized good object. The twin figure "represents those un-understood and split off parts which the individual is longing to regain, in the hope of achieving wholeness and complete understanding; they are sometimes felt to be the ideal parts."[16]

Shelley's fantasized maiden / self is perhaps that whole self, that loved self, never bestowed by or received from the mother. But because this self is only fantasy, because it is too closely tied to the ambivalently split, threatening mother, a complete union or identification with it is inevitably doomed. Shelley's description of erotic union with the maiden expresses a fantasy of regressive fusion which leads only to death. When the Poet, "sickened with excess of love," is "folded" in the maiden's "dissolving arms," Shelley describes how "blackness veiled his dizzy eyes, and night / Involved and swallowed up the vision" (181-91). The specifically oral nature of the imagery here again betrays the schizoid-narcissistic condition of a love so hungry that the overriding fear is that both the object and the self will be consumed in one terrifying annihilation.

With the disappearance of the visionary maiden, the landscape becomes increasingly desolate and the tone increasingly desperate. The repetition of the very words *despair* and *desolate* reinforces that condition of hopeless futility which is the mark of the narcissist's internally severed world. The attitude and tone of the entire poem is perhaps best summed up by the impassioned exclamation,

> . . . Alas! Alas!
> Were limbs, and breath, and being intertwined
> Thus treacherously? Lost, lost, forever lost,
> In the wide pathless desert of dim sleep,
> That beautiful shape!
>
> [207-11]

Finally, after the Poet despairs of ever recovering the lost vision of his soul in life, the remainder of the poem describes his direct and determined movement toward death: "A restless impulse urged him to embark / And meet lone Death on the drear Ocean's waste" (304-5). Death, as Havens observed, becomes the "doorway for reunion." The Poet's desire for death reveals that desire for regressive fusion which Kernberg points to as one of the most profound characteristics of the narcissistic personality. The Poet approaches death as Beatrice at the end of *The Cenci* welcomes Death's "all-embracing arms" and appeals to Death "like a fond mother" to "hide me in thy bosom, / And rock me to the sleep from which none wake" (5, 4, 117-18). For Shelley, death is a remerging, a denial of separateness and reality.

Finally, toward the end of the poem, the Poet arrives at a well in which he beholds his own image, "As the human heart, / Gazing in dreams over the gloomy grave, / Sees its own treacherous likeness there" (472-73). Like the ideal maiden/self, the image is "treacherous" and associated with death. The focus of the image here is the "two eyes, / Two starry eyes," which "hung in the gloom of thought, / And seemed with their serene and azure smiles / To beckon him" (489-92). The stars are "the light / That shone within his soul"; they are, like the ideal mate, the ideal reflection of the self. These symbolic reflecting eyes recall Kohut's contention that the child first identifies and confirms himself as he is "mirrored" by the gleam in his mother's eyes.[17] And stars, being constant and eternal, provide a frequent symbol for Shelley of that fixed identity, of the "real" self that is being sought. The famous concluding image of *Adonais*, in which "The soul of Adonais, like a star, / Beacons from the abode where the Eternal are," underscores an interpretation of the poet-figure in that poem, too, as essentially a reflection of a lost, ideal self.

The moon in *Alastor* provides one other significant image; it is always associated with the mother, and specifically with the breast:

> The dim and horned moon hung low, and poured
> A sea of luster on the horizon's verge
> That overflowed its mountains. Yellow mist
> Filled the unbounded atmosphere, and drank
> Wan moonlight even to fullness: . . .
>
> [602-6]

The Poet's final vision as he draws his last breath is, in fact, of the moon—"his last sight / Was the great moon"—and the two stars —"two lessening points of light alone / Gleamed through the darkness." The heaven ultimately turns "utterly black," however, and the Poet, only an image now, is "involved" by the "murky shades" and is as "silent, cold and motionless" as the "voiceless earth and vacant air" (660-62). He is "Still, dark, and unremembered now." He can "no longer know or love the shapes / Of this phantasmal scene," and nothing remains "But pale despair and cold tranquility." Thus, the final vision is of a phantasmal and unreal life, utterly desolate and futile. Although Shelley gives evidence in the preface of apparently recognizing the inherent dangers and unhealthiness of his poem—the Poet, he says, "was avenged" for his "self-centered seclusion"—in the poem itself this perspective is never realized. The infantile fears and fantasies and the embittered self-pity are never lifted.

The vacancy, the void with which *Alastor* concludes, expresses the subjective experience of the loss of an integrated relationship between the self and its world of internal objects. As Kernberg explains, the lack of an integrated self is characterized by feelings of unreality and emptiness and by an incapacity to perceive oneself realistically as a total human being. The human world, he says, will seem emptied of meaning, of meaningful, loving relationships, and "the world of inanimate objects will seem sharply delimited, looming or protruding from the usual surrounding."[18] The environ-

ment will convey a quality of impenetrability. I am reminded of
Shelley's description of the "solid air" and the "solid darkness" in
Lines written among the Euganean Hills; of "This dim vast vale of
tears, vacant and desolate" in *Hymn to Intellectual Beauty;* of the
"dead, blank cold air" in *Epipsychidion;* and of Laon's nightmare
in *The Revolt of Islam:*

> A gulf, a void, a sense of senselessness —
>   These things dwelt in me, even as shadows keep
> Their watch in some dim charnel's loneliness,
> A shoreless sea, a sky sunless and planetless!
> . . . .
> Foul, ceaseless shadows: — thought could not divide
>   The actual world from these entangling evils,
> Which so bemocked themselves, that I descried
> All shapes like mine own self, hideously multiplied.
>   [1302-5, 1311-14]

   Shelley's poetry, more powerfully than any clinical description,
portrays the pathological condition of a fragmented self. "A gulf,
a void, a sense of senselessness" pervades the picture of both the
internal and external world in his poetry. There is indeed a general
confusion between the internal and external, an inability to separate the "actual world" from the "entangling evils" of inner fantasy.
The external environment in his poetry is always portrayed as
untrustworthy, often as erupting violently. His frequent images of
mountains cracking or of floods breaking through chasms betray
severe internal disruption. Finally, the relation of this fragmented
condition to its source in an intense ambivalence is perhaps no-
where better revealed than in the following passage from *Epipsychidion:*

> What storms then shook the ocean of my sleep,
> Blotting that Moon, whose pale and waning lips
> Then shrank as in the sickness of eclipse; —
> And how my soul was a lampless sea,
> And who was then its Tempest; and when She,
> The Planet of that hour, was quenched, what frost
> Crept o'er those waters, till from coast to coast
> The moving billows of my being fell
> Into a death of ice, immovable; —

And then—what earthquakes made it gape and split,
The white Moon smiling all the while on it,

[307-18]

First, there is the destructive fantasy—the storms "Blotting" the feminine Moon, which shrinks in sickness—and then the fearsome retaliation—the "death of ice" and the earthquakes—while a sadistic Moon is "smiling all the while on it."

Thundering storms, wrenching earthquakes, and fierce, retaliatory female figures are also typical of Blake's poetry. Two of his shorter lyrics, *The Mental Traveller* and *The Crystal Cabinet*, in fact share the *Alastor* theme of quest for an elusive and treacherous ideal maiden. *The Mental Traveller* is filled with images of feeding and drinking, of sucking and vampire love. The traveler at one point finds a maiden, takes her in his arms, and the world "fades" and shrinks away, becoming "a desert vast" with "nothing left to eat or drink." But then the maiden feeds him with "the honey of her lips" and the "bread and wine" of her smile, and so "Does him to Infancy beguile." She disappears and he grows younger still, wandering through the desert in "terror, and dismay," pursuing her through labyrinths and thickets until finally he becomes, as he is at the beginning of the poem, a "frowning babe" whom none can touch except the Woman Old, who nails him down upon a rock. *The Crystal Cabinet* tells the same story. When the speaker attempts to "seize the inmost Form" of the maiden, he bursts the cabinet and becomes "A weeping Babe upon the wild / And weeping Woman pale reclined / And in the outward air again / I filled with woes the passing Wind." Like the mental traveler, he fails to embrace or unite with the woman, he regresses to an abandoned infant, and the elusive shadowy woman "reclines" and deserts him. Like the Poet in *Alastor*, he is alone in an unresponsive, echoless world.

This schizoid-narcissistic condition also underlies what critics frequently refer to as Shelley's philosophic Platonism. Shelley's feeling that reality is hidden, veiled, elusive—that "Power dwells apart in its tranquility, / Remote, serene and inaccessible" (*Mont Blanc*, ll. 96-97) is in essence only a variation of the *Alastor* theme. The remote, inaccessible Power that dwells apart in an ideal realm is the same remote, inaccessible Nature in *Alastor*, the same remote and inaccessible ideal maiden. As an infant's entire existence depends upon the mother, her power is indeed the foremost reality of its life. Shelley's frustrated and unresolved relationship with his first maternal environment colors his conception of the environment, of external reality, throughout his poetry. The relationship is also at the base of his overall poetic style, as Storch observes. Storch labels Shelley's style "abstract idealism"—abstract because it "tends to lose touch with the concrete (grown together) realities, and tends to see objects in disjunction, revealing a separation of subject and object."[19] From *Alastor* to *The Triumph of Life*, Shelley's poetry expresses this disjunction, portraying a fragmented self and a fragmented world. Bloom notes that Shelley's quest "comes full circle from 'Alastor' to 'The Triumph of Life,'" and he even compares the total structure of Shelley's poetic canon to the ironic cycle of Blake's *Mental Traveller*.[20] The comparison seems apt, but considering the mental traveler's infantile, dissolute and desperate state, the "full circle" seems a dubious achievement.

THE TRIUMPH OF LIFE: THE QUEST ONCE MORE

In approaching the ironically titled *Triumph of Life*, critics often begin by sedulously tracing the influence of Dante, apparent in the poem's imagery and terza rima scheme. Although the influence is certainly there, I find the overall imagery and thematic progression less derivative than typically Shelleyan. The winged chariot, for instance, may have a source in *The Purgatorio*, but it also figures in some form in most of Shelley's major poems. The image has particular associations and meaning as it belongs to the particular psychology of Shelley's imagination. *The Triumph* is another form, another expression, of the same emotional conflicts that shape *Alastor*. Although unfinished, the poem yet presents a vision of defeat and despair which is total. Donald Reiman, who has written the most extensive study of the poem, says that it is about the "conquest and destruction of human moral freedom" by "natural necessity." The Car of Life, he says, symbolizes external, arbitrary power.[21] I would state it more simply and, I believe, precisely: the poem portrays Life as an external, specifically female power that is treacherous and destructive. The female images in *The Triumph* reflect the same intense ambivalence as they do in *Alastor*, and, as in the earlier poem, the woman both tantalizes and thwarts the sensitive, outcast poet-figure. What Reiman calls "this sad reality" (p. 19) of the human situation is more precisely the sad reality of the schizoid-narcissistic personality. Shelley's Life, what he portrays as reality, is only the reality of an infantile, unintegrated self who is actually incapable of accepting the reality of aloneness and death and incapable of knowing the reality of a nondestructive love.

The Triumph opens with a celebration of the rising sun, a rare moment in a poem that otherwise expresses little but embittered anguish and despair. The most significant aspect of the sun in this passage is its powerfully assertive, specifically paternal character: "the Sun sprang forth / Rejoicing in his splendor," and all the earth, "Isle, ocean, and all things . . . / Rise as the Sun their father rose. . . ." All things rise, that is, but the narrator—"But I, whom thoughts which must remain untold / Had kept as wakeful as the stars. . . ." The narrator is unable to identify or ally himself with the father; he is unable to realize or fully assert his male identity. Rather, he feels thwarted, troubled by "untold" thoughts. The source of his frustration lies in the vision that he proceeds to describe.

In this vision, or "waking dream," the narrator sees himself beside a public way, witnessing "a great stream / Of people . . . hurrying to and fro, / Numerous as gnats upon the evening gleam. . . ." The people are frantic and chaotic—"none seemed to know / Whither he went, or whence he came, or why / He made one of the multitude, . . ." (44-49). This dream is more precisely a nightmare, the affective content being terror:

> Old age and youth, manhood and infancy,
>
> Mixed in one mighty torrent did appear,
> Some flying from the thing they feared, and some
> Seeking the object of another's fear;
>
> And others, as with steps towards the tomb,
> Pored on the trodden worms that crawled beneath,
> And others mournfully within the gloom
>
> Of their own shadow walked, and called it death;
> And some fled from it as it were a ghost,
> Half fainting in the affliction of vain breath
>
> [52-61]

The trampling crowd rushing with fear perhaps expresses an over-powering upsurge of the narrator's, or Shelley's, own unconscious violent and terrifying feelings. The trampling, the morbid gloom, and the representation of the people as confused and shadowy are all typical Shelleyan images; together they compose a vision of that persecutory and terrifying internal world of the narcissist. The images reflect the narcissist's deepest feelings of violent, un-controllable rage as well as a fear of being overcome and de-stroyed by that rage. The shadowy, confused figures betray the inability to feel oneself or to perceive others as bodily and co-herent, as a substantial reality. The vision of such a ghostly, crushing multitude echoes Laon's nightmare in *The Revolt of Islam* in which "Foul, ceaseless shadows" sweep upon him in "a giddy dance" and in which he recognizes "shapes like mine own self, hideously multiplied." The vision also recalls the opening of *Ode to the West Wind*, in which the dead leaves are described as "ghosts from an enchanger fleeing," as "Pestilence-striken multi-tudes" whom the West Wind "chariotest" to their graves. A be-witching, death-driving chariot, as will be discussed, lies behind the rushing multitudes in *The Triumph* as well. Shelley's deepest terror always takes the form of being crushed, trampled—Death indeed "tramples" the multicolored glass dome of Life in *Adonais*. At the source of this terror of being trampled and overpowered is the omnipotent, terrifying mother imago, which *The Triumph* makes abundantly clear.

As the throng grows wilder, Shelley describes a "cold glare" that intensifies and finally "obscure[s] with blinding light / The sun." This icy, blinding light, one learns, is caused by the "rushing splendour" of a great chariot, carrying within it a "Shape." Shelley introduces the image with the analogy of the "young moon," which bears, as the herald of its coming, "The ghost of its dead mother." The association of the Shape in the chariot with the dead mother is telling, as is the description of the Shape "as one whom years deform, / Beneath a dusky hood and double cape, / Crouch-ing within the shadow of a tomb" (87-90). Not only does the Shape suggest the dead mother, or a mother who symbolically embodies death, but the winged chariot itself, as appears repeatedly in Shelley's poetry, suggests the maternal womb. Here womb and tomb are synonymous. Thus, the familiar ambivalent mother is now seen as the cause of that trampling multitude, or, in emotional terms, as the source of that upsurge of enraged and terrifying feelings.

Shelley stresses repeatedly how the chariot "obscures," "quenches," and "dims the sun." The ambivalent mother imago is obstructing or preventing the poet from realizing his male identity. His inability to realize himself is inextricably tied to his inability to perceive the mother as a substantial realistic whole. His intense ambivalence keeps her ghostly and split—she is "a dun and faint aethereal gloom" who is being driven by a "Janus-visaged Shadow." The four faces of the Charioteer significantly have "their eyes banded," an ironic twist, as Bloom points out, of the traditional "innumerable eyes" of the four-faced cherubim. The chariot speeds blindly yet "majestically" on, and before the poet "can say *where*—the chariot hath / Passed over" the crowd.

It is particularly significant, and horrifying for Shelley, that the great chariot rolls over the people without seeing them. From a psychological viewpoint, the image portrays the mother as blind, as incapable of perceiving or realizing the existence of the child. The image of a sightless, unreflecting mother also figures prominently, as I shall discuss later, in the poetry of Keats and Coleridge. The image suggests, in Kohut's terms, a failure in the earliest "mirroring" relationship between the self and the mother. From the beginning, Kohut says, the infant self needs to feel acknowledged and "reflected" by that first love object with whom it is so powerfully and deeply intertwined. Failure in this early mirroring relationship can prevent the normal development of an autonomous integrated self.

Shelley's image of Life as a formless, specifically sightless presence occurs again in a sonnet published with the *Posthumous Poems* (1824):

> Lift not the painted veil which those who live
> Call life: though unreal shapes be pictured there,
> And it but mimic all we would believe
> With colours idly spread,—behind, lurk Fear
> And Hope, twin Destinies; who ever weave
> Their shadows, o'er the chasm, sightless and drear.
> I knew one who had lifted it—he sought,
> For his lost heart was tender, things to love,
> But found them not, alas! nor was there aught

The world contains, the which he could approve.
Through the unheeding many he did move,
A splendour among the shadows, a bright blot
Upon this gloomy scene, a Spirit that strove
For truth, and like the Preacher found it not.

Like the hooded Shape in the chariot, the image of Life is veiled
and shadowy, "sightless" and "drear," an empty "chasm" that
inspires both Hope and Fear, desire and terror. The "I" of the
sonnet, furthermore, is typically shadowy and unformed; he describes himself as "A splendour among shadows, a bright blot"
who dares to lift the veil in search of "things to love, / But found
them not, alas!"

The chariot in *The Triumph* inspires the same extreme ambivalence and it, too, leads only to destruction and desolation for the
shadowy figures who pursue it. Shelley describes the followers as
being

Like moths by light attracted and repelled,
Oft to their bright destruction come and go,
Till like two clouds into one vale impelled,
That shake the mountains when their lightenings mingle
And die in rain . . .

[153-57]

The description also betrays images of regressive fusion—the
clouds that merge so that their "lightenings mingle and die," as, a
few lines earlier, Shelley describes the youths and maidens "Bending within each other's atmosphere" (151). The images of erotic
fusion ultimately dissolve, as they always do in Shelley's poetry,
into images of death and desolation: the chariot vanishes leaving
only a trace "as of foam after the ocean's wrath / Is spent upon the
desert shore" (163-64) and the men and women, with "limbs de-
cayed," sink back into the dust.

The narrator, left standing amidst the ruins, cries, "And what
is this / Whose shape is that within the car?" to which a voice
answers, "Life." The voice, one learns, belongs to the ancient and
decrepit figure of Rousseau, whose history occupies the remainder
of the poem. Rousseau's story provides merely one more version
of the sad *Alastor* tale of wounded narcissism and unresolved
ambivalence. He explains, first of all, that all the figures chained to

the car are "The wise, / The great, the unforgotten" (209) who waged a battle with Life, but "She remained conqueror." He, on the other hand, "was overcome / By my own heart alone, which neither age, / Nor tears, nor infamy, nor now the tomb / Could temper to its object" (240-43). As Rousseau then describes the most formative event in his past life, one discovers that the battle waged within his own heart is the same as that waged by those chained to the car; that "object" to which his heart could not be "tempered" is the ideal/destructive omnipotent mother imago.

Rousseau describes how, one April past, he was "laid asleep" beneath a mountain, in

> a cavern high and deep;
> And from it came a gentle rivulet,
> Whose water, like clear air, in its calm sleep
> Bent the soft grass, and kept for ever wet
> The stems of the sweet flowers, . . .
>
> [313-18]

For Rousseau, the most desirable aspect of this womblike environment is the oblivion it brings; it makes one "forget / All pleasure and all pain, all hate and love, / Which they had known before that hour of rest" (318-20). This desire to escape the "harsh world" by a regressive return to the womb is a recurring motif in Shelley's poetry, as I have noted. Rousseau's cavern promises the same sweet oblivion as the undecaying "green hermitage," which is "beyond the rage of death or life" in *The Witch of Atlas*, or as the "windless bower," which is "Far from passion, pain and guilt" in *Lines written among the Euganean Hills*. Rousseau indeed calls his sleep an "oblivious spell" that, upon waking, casts a "diviner" light on the earth and fills his ears with an "oblivious melody."

Rousseau's next vision is of "A Shape all light . . . as if she were the dawn"—a fair, tender, splendid creature who glides along the air raining sweet dew on the earth—an image, by now familiar, of the ideal mother. As usual, however, Shelley cannot keep her ideal for long; the sweetly diaphanous lady soon reveals a more sinister aspect. Shelley describes how her feet

> . . . seemed as they moved to blot
> The thoughts of him who gazed on them; and soon

All that was, seemed as if it had been not;
And all the gazer's mind was strewn beneath
Her feet like embers; and she, thought by thought,

Trampled its sparks into the dust of death

[382-88]

Again, Shelley's fear of the woman's phallic and destructive power
to trample upon, to "blot" out and annihilate the self is evident.
Rousseau describes how he felt "Suspended," as "one between
desire and shame." He was paralyzed by his ambivalence, unable
to assert himself. As the Poet in *Alastor* seeks for his identity in
the images of Nature/mother and the ideal maiden, so Rousseau
implored his ideal lady to "Show whence I came, and where I am,
and why—" (398). In reply, she offered to "quench" his thirst, but
as soon as his lips touched the cup, his "brain became as sand,"
and a new vision burst upon his sight, and "the fair shape waned
in the coming light, / As veil by veil the silent splendour drops /
From Lucifer" (405, 412-13). The scene, remarkably reminiscent of
Blake's *Mental Traveller*, describes the experience of desolation at
the breast, the experience at the psychological core of the poem.

Although the vision of the ideal woman now dims, Rousseau
describes how her shape, like "The ghost of a forgotten form of
sleep; / A light of heaven, whose half-extinguished beam / Through
the sick day in which we wake to weep / Glimmers, for ever
sought, for ever lost" (428-31). The passage parallels Wordsworth's
description of the "clouds of glory" which the infant trails with
him into this world, the glowing dream of the lost harmony and
oneness with the mother. Whereas Wordsworth is able to confront
the loss and integrate it into a larger, more mature vision of
experience, Shelley is unable to relinquish the dream or resolve its
loss. He is unable to come to terms with his ambivalent ties to the
mother. Thus, a new vision of a terrible "cold bright car" super-
cedes the ideal one of old. Rousseau is "borne onward" by the
chariot, swept on "among the multitude." In a fury of self-pity, he
protests his exposed and violated self:

        —I among the multitude
Was swept—me, sweetest flowers delayed not long;
Me, not the shadow nor the solitude;

Me, not that falling stream's Lethean song;
Me, not the phantom of that early Form
Which moved upon its motion — but among

The thickest billows of that living storm
I plunged, and bared my bosom to the clime
Of that cold light, whose airs too soon deform.

[460-68]

The remainder of the poem describes an atmosphere of increasing diffusion and disintegration. The air thickens with "shadows," "phantoms," "vampire-bats," apes and monsters with "dead eyes." All beauty, strength, and freshness wanes and dies, and Rousseau concludes, "Then, what is life? I cried." Indeed, what is life for the disintegrated self but a continual experience of formless rage, overwhelming terror, and hopeless idealistic yearning? Unable to confront or resolve his intense feelings of rage and aggression toward the mother, or to give up his deep need to be completely and perfectly fused with her, Shelley remains incapable of portraying a mature experience of reality in his poetry. One can turn to Shelley's actual relationships for confirmation of these narcissistic patterns of idealization and consequent disillusionment. He was well known for his extreme and violent shifts of opinion about people, especially in regard to women. In his aborted relationships with Harriet Westbrook, Elizabeth Hutchinson, Mary Godwin, and Jane Williams, among others, Shelley betrayed an incapacity to trust or remain faithful to any one woman for long. The delusions of persecution and the hallucinations that haunted him toward the end of his life (particularly striking is his fantasy of seeing eyes in Mary Godwin's nipples) suggest the disorders of a personality self-destructively attached to the image of the mother.

Only *Ode to the West Wind*, to my mind Shelley's finest poem, manages to accept a painful reality that includes both love and loss at once. By objectifying and confronting the Wind as "Destroyer and preserver" both, Shelley is able to confront his own ambivalent feelings toward that tantalizing and treacherous parent in whose "unseen presence" he has been like a dead leaf, a ghost "from an enchanter fleeing." Although the poem threatens at one point to collapse into characteristic self-pity — "Oh, lift me

as a wave, a leaf, a cloud! / I fall upon the thorns of life! I bleed!"
—it then moves into a more mature acceptance:

> Make me thy lyre, even as the forest is:
> What if my leaves are falling like its own!
> The tumult of thy mighty harmonies
>
> Will take from both a deep, autumnal tone,
> Sweet though in sadness . . . .
>
> [57-61]

Love and death are one in the spirit of the Wind, and Shelley
identifies with it. He accepts this spirit within himself and charges
it to "Drive my dead thoughts over the universe / Like withered
leaves to quicken a new birth!" The poet is liberated by his sudden
acceptance of a reality that includes destruction and loss and by
his acceptance of those same loving and destructive feelings in
himself. The objective form of the poem allows a distance from,
and yet an expression of, the painful emotions. The unity achieved
in the poetic form reflects, at least momentarily, a unification
achieved in the personality.

In conclusion, the *Alastor* quest, the hopeless search of the
wounded narcissist for his ideal maiden/self, is the most central
shaping situation of Shelley's poetry. The figure of the wounded
narcissist is itself characteristically Romantic. This by no means
implies that most Romantic poetry is as characteristically and
regressively narcissistic as *Alastor*. The most successful Romantic
poems display the effort involved in resisting a regressive tendency
toward narcissistic idealization, fusion, and dissolution. They
portray the struggle to confront feelings that are at once loving
and destructive, and to accept a single, complex reality that, like
the West Wind, includes both love and loss.

·2·
KEATS

INTRODUCTION

The images of women in Keats's poetry are well known for their ambivalent character. The famous *La Belle Dame sans Merci*, for instance, beguiles the innocent knight with her beauty and charm, feeding him on sweets and relishes, only to leave him, as she has many others, with "starved lips," "Alone and palely loitering," on a "withered" and "cold hill's side." Although *La Belle Dame* depicts the experience of oral deprivation, portraying a withdrawing and denying mother, *Lamia* reveals an even more overtly hostile and aggressive attitude toward both the woman and the self. The serpent-woman tantalizes and entices the young Lycius, who loves her in "self despite / Against his better self," and both are ultimately destroyed. Like so many of Byron's heroes, Lycius is victim not only of the woman's ambivalent nature but also of his own. He loves in "self despite"; the destructive rage is located in the self, in the nature of his own love as well as in the woman's. Perhaps no lines express Keats's attitude toward women more openly and urgently than those of the following sonnet, written in desperation to Fanny toward the end of his life:

> I cry your mercy—pity—love! aye, love!
>   Merciful love that tantalizes not,
> One-thoughted, never-wandering, guileless love,
>   Unmask'd, and being seen—without a blot!

O! let me have thee whole,—all—all—be mine!
    That shape, that fairness, that sweet minor zest
Of love, your kiss,—those hands, those eyes divine
    That warm, white, lucent, million-pleasured breast,—
Yourself—your soul—in pity give me all,
    Withhold no atom's atom or I die,
Or living on perhaps, your wretched thrall,
    Forget, in the mist of idle misery,
Life's purposes,—the palate of my mind
Losing its gust, and my ambition blind!

The sonnet betrays an intense mistrust of the woman's love as well as an intense need to wholly possess the woman, to consume or incorporate her. Critics have indeed noted the pervasive strain of oral imagery in Keats's poetry. Certainly Yeats's well-known description of Keats as a young boy with his nose pressed up against a candy shop window betrays at least an intuitive recognition of the infantile oral greed so definitive of Keats's personality. Trilling, too, has commented on the extreme and pervasive ingestive imagery in Keats's poetry.[1] The critics have failed to recognize, however, the vital connection between this oral disposition of the personality and the major themes of Keats's work in general—the idealism, the aestheticism, and the preoccupation with identity. In the above sonnet, for instance, the fact that Keats should refer to his mind in oral terms, as a palate losing its gust, suggests the relevance of the oral experience to Keats's entire self-concept. Or again, in a letter (April 21, 1819), Keats refers to the heart as "the teat from which the mind or intelligence sucks its identity." The imagery suggests an intuitive grasp of the deep relation of the earliest breast experience to the formation of a coherent identity or self.

Trilling, in fact, sees the oral experience in Keats's work as evidence of a positive strength of personality. Keats's preoccupation with this most primitive of the appetites, Trilling maintains, suggests that he "did not repress the infantile wish; he confronted it, recognized it, and delighted in it." It is we, he says, not Keats, who are ambivalent about it. Trilling speaks of the strong, direct, and "genial" relations of the Keats family and of the "generous" and "indulgent" nature of the mother. The few known facts about Keats's mother, however, suggest an at least equally selfish and irresponsible nature.[2] More importantly, though, why should Keats be so preoccupied in his poetry with what Trilling calls a felicity of maternal "dainties, kisses and coziness" (p. 21) if, as a child, he had been completely satisfied and fulfilled? If Trilling's claim that Keats's indulged childhood enabled him to "bid these joys farewell" and "leave them for a nobler life" is true (p. 23), why then does the poetry repeatedly express the desire to retreat into a womblike ideal world? Why is it so preoccupied with a paradisical bliss in such oral, infantile terms? Although the poetry does display a developing strength, an increasing ability to relinquish this idealized infantile bliss, it always reveals the extreme difficulty for Keats, the intense struggle involved in doing so. In his finest poems, such as *Ode to a Nightingale* and *To Autumn*, Keats does succeed in bidding these joys farewell.

Whereas Trilling points to the oral experience in Keats's poetry as evidence of a heroic strength of personality, Arthur Wormhoudt sees it as evidence of a passive masochistic personality.[3] Wormhoudt, in fact, believes an unresolved masochistic attachment to the image of the mother lies at the base of all Romantic poetry, and that any display of aggression functions merely as a defensive denial of this attachment. I find most of Wormhoudt's analyses too strained and extreme. Neither Trilling's nor Wormhoudt's interpretation is completely satisfactory in itself. Although the oral element in Keats's poetry is not, as Trilling insists, evidence of personal strength, the poetry often does exhibit a heroic assertiveness that is not merely a defensive denial.

The oral character of Keats's poetry, first of all, is everywhere indicative of a regressive narcissistic hunger, ambivalence, and desire for refusion. In *The Eve of St. Agnes*, for instance, several stanzas are devoted to the delicious edibles and delicacies heaped in Madeline's bedchamber, and this oral eroticism occurs along with images of the two young lovers melting and blending with each other and with the poem's overall fantasy of escape. Frequently, the idea of swooning to death, or of fading and dissolving, accompanies the oral/breast image. In the sonnet *Bright Star*, for example, the poet asks to live forever "Pillow'd upon my fair love's ripening breast / . . .—or else swoon to death," and in *Ode to a Nightingale* he longs for a "draught of vintage" so that he might drink and "fade away," "dissolve," and "forget." *Sleep and Poetry* also equates feasting with love. Moreover, the verse expresses the desire to retreat into an ideal maternal world—"Till in the bosom of a leafy world / We rest in silence, like two gems

upcurl'd / In the recesses of a pearly shell" (119-21)—while also
betraying a note of sadistic oral hostility: the poet wishes to kiss
and woo the nymphs, to "touch their shoulders white / Into a
pretty shrinking with a bite / As hard as lips can make it . . ."
(107-9). As discussed, the desire for regressive refusion with the
mother is necessarily accompanied by an intense ambivalence. As
much as Keats yearns to become fused, dissolved, or absorbed in
his loved one, he also fears an annihilation of his self. In a letter
(July 25, 1819) he cries to Fanny, "You absorb me in spite of
myself!"

In both the poetry and the letters, however, Keats frequently
displays a strong resistance against such an annihilating passive
refusion. Although the images of women are usually associated
with the experience of infantile oral eroticism, with a passive,
luxurious abandonment of the self to idealized fantasy and death,
these experiences are often countered by an aggressive effort to
assert the self and to remain in reality. This is perhaps what Trilling
means when he claims that Keats institutes "a kind of antagonism
between the idea of luxury and the idea of energetic morality"
(p. 24). As much as Keats claims that poets have no identity, and
that when he is in a room with people "the identity of everyone in
the room begins to press upon me that, I am in a very little time
annihilated" (October 27, 1818), he nevertheless comes to realize
that the ability of the poet or genius to "lose" personal identity, to
expand and surrender the self, must depend at bottom on an ex-
ceptionally strong identity or self. In the letter (April 21, 1819) in
which Keats describes the world as a "vale of Soul-making," he
argues that souls are distinguished from pure "intelligences" by
virtue of their "identities . . . each one is personally itself." This
"identity," a "bliss peculiar to each one's individual existence," is
acquired through the interrelationship of three elements: the intelligence, the heart, and the world. The intelligence and the heart
must be schooled by a "World of pains and troubles" in order to
become a soul. Keats concludes:

> I began by seeing how man was formed by circumstances—and
> what are circumstances?—but touchstones of his heart—? and
> what are proovings of his heart but fortifiers or alterers of his
> nature? and what is his altered nature but his soul?—and what
> was his soul before it came into the world and had these proov-

ings and alterations and perfectionings?—An intelligence without Identity—and how is this Identity to be made? Through the medium of the Heart. And how is the heart to become this Medium but in a world of Circumstances?[4]

Thus, while Keats can speak of having no identity and no self, he yet recognizes that personal identity—the identity formed by our affective relationships with objects in the world outside ourselves— is an essential and vital determinant of our specifically human nature.

Finally, Keats's poetic style itself, its concreteness and tactility, suggests, as F. R. Leavis has observed, "a strong grasp upon actualities," a firm sense of the solid world, "of things outside himself."[5] This ability to see the world as concrete, solid, and coherent is contingent, as discussed in the first chapter, on an ability to love maturely. The child must resolve its narcissistic and ambivalent relationship with its first maternal environment, it must accept the mother as whole, separate and "lost," if it is ever to perceive a reality that is separate, concrete, and outside itself. Keats's poetry thus exhibits a dynamic tension not present in Shelley's poetry; the tendency toward regressive refusion and toward narcissistic fantasy and idealization is frequently checked by an equally intense desire to confront reality, to accept its "otherness," and to establish mature object relations.

Aileen Ward's *John Keats* offers a good basis from which to begin a psychological examination of the poetry. She discusses the instability of Keats's early family life—the death of his father when Keats was eight, the mother's remarriage two months later and her subsequent mysterious disappearance for several years, and finally the mother's return home where she was to die when Keats was fourteen. As a result, Ward claims, Keats felt deeply betrayed and abandoned by his mother.[6] Ward notes Keats's remark in one of the letters, "All my life I have suspected every Body." She concludes that Keats's loss of his father at a crucial age for identification with the male parent and the loss of the mother again at a time of sexual reawakening "laid a burden of emotion on him which would later seek an outlet." Poetry eventually pointed out for him "a road back to the lost paradise of sensuous and emotional delight" and it also became a "kind of communication with the immortal dead" (p. 40).

I agree that the death of the parents must have been profound
and traumatic events in Keats's young life, but I would not go so
far as Ward to explain the entire disposition of his personality on
the two actual events themselves. For as discussed in the first
chapter, it is generally recognized in clinical psychoanalysis today
that the structure of the self is determined far earlier than the
eighth year; the most formative period of personality development
occurs during the first year, indeed during the first few months of
life. Although the death of a parent can certainly reactivate and
intensify former ambivalence and trauma, the event in itself cannot
be solely responsible for a personality that, as Ward observes,
lacks a clear image of its self (p. 52) or that, as Keats himself observed, is continually "full of suspicion" of "evil thoughts, malice
and spleen" when in the company of women (Keats to Bailey,
July 18, 1818). Thus, that aspect of the poetry which Ward interprets as an attempt to communicate with or recover the dead
mother can, from a contemporary psychoanalytic perspective,
assume a deeper, less literal and limited meaning. The poetry expresses a struggle to relate to a mother who is not only literally
dead, but who was affectively experienced as dead—indifferent,
untrustworthy, unloving—by the infant self. This experience, as
we have seen, can have acute and far-reaching effects on the developing personality. The infant's experience of the mother as its
earliest love object deeply influences its experience of itself as a
whole, coherent identity and its ability to perceive reality. Keats's
Endymion, his first poem of any consequence, deals precisely with
these themes; it explores the vital connection of one's love relationships to one's growing realization of self and reality.

ENDYMION:
KEATS'S *ALASTOR*

Harold Bloom claims that *Endymion* is "our fullest revelation
of the reach and power of Keats's poetic mind." Although that is a
decided overestimation of the poem, most critics do agree on the
importance of *Endymion* to an understanding of the body of
Keats's work. As Bruce Miller points out, in *Endymion* Keats
"reveals himself more openly than in any of his other work."[7] Like
Alastor, *Endymion* tells the tale of a young poet's pursuit after an
elusive ideal goddess. Although the critics all interpret the tale as

an allegorical or symbolic quest, they cannot agree, as with *Alastor*, as to the exact nature and meaning of that quest.

In reviewing the criticism on the poem, Miller sees the various interpretations as falling into two general categories: a Neoplatonic view that focuses on the poet's communion with an ideal beauty, love, or truth and stresses the visionary, spiritual aspects of the poem; and a perspective that highlights the physical, passionate, sensual qualities of the poem and claims that it is primarily about erotic love. Miller himself attempts to incorporate both perspectives in his interpretation by separating reality into the natural and supernatural and arguing that in the poem, love becomes the conjunction between the two. He talks about love as an "escape" of the self, as a "merging" and "fusing" (p. 42). John Middleton Murry also argues that the poem is about the fusing power of love and that the poet, through his experience of various kinds of love, is able to reconcile "the contradictory passions of the Heart"—the passion of the soul and the passion of the body.[8] Both Miller's and Murry's interpretations, however, simply assume a split condition in either the nature of reality or in the nature of the human heart. Neither explains precisely how and why the poet's experience of love leads to the actual resolution of this split at the end. A psychoanalytic examination of the poem can offer insight into the nature of this split condition, into the poem's dual strains of idealism and sensuality, and can also account, in more concrete, human terms, for the poet's reconciliation at the end.

In brief outline, the story of *Endymion* goes as follows: Book 1 describes the young poet Endymion in a state of sickness and distraction as he pines for love of the ravishing moon-goddess who has thrice appeared to him in his dreams; Book 2 traces his descent into the earth as he winds his way through caves, palaces and subterranean streams in search of his elusive goddess; Book 3 tells of his encounter under the sea with the old man Glaucus who, like Endymion, pursued an ideal love (the sea-nymph Scylla) and is consequently suffering under the spell of the cruel and jealous Circe. Endymion, his "twin brother in this destiny," has been fated to break the spell. Finally, Book 4 introduces the sorrowful Indian maid whose mortal love Endymion is at last able to accept and, for this acceptance, he is ultimately rewarded by the maid's transformation into the goddess at the end. A careful examination of the specific imagery in this often diffuse and seemingly incoherent poem uncovers a distinct psychological coherence.

The poem opens with Keats's famous declaration,

> A thing of beauty is a joy for ever:
> Its loveliness increases; it will never
> Pass into nothingness; but still will keep
> A bower quiet for us, and a sleep
> Full of sweet dreams, and health, and quiet breathing.

Our entire understanding of the poem, in fact, will largely depend on our understanding of what exactly Keats means by the word "beauty" here. In these first stanzas, his "beauty" is not only a "bower" and a "sleep" but also "some shape" that "moves away the pall from our dark spirits" (12-13). It is both sensuous and earthly—"Such the sun, the moon, / Trees old, and young, sprouting a shady boon / For simple sheep; and such are daffodils / With the green world they live in" (13-17)—and also "An endless fountain of immortal drink / Pouring into us from the heaven's brink" (23-24). Those critics who interpret *Endymion* as a Neoplatonic allegory focus on this eternal and divine quality Keats ascribes to beauty and on his conception of it as a "shape," an ideal, an "essence":

> Nor do we merely feel these essences
> For one short hour; no, even as the trees
> That whisper round a temple become soon
> Dear as the temple's self, so does the moon,
> The passion poesy, glories infinite,
> Haunt us till they become a cheering light
> Unto our souls, and bound to us so fast,
> That, whether there be shine, or gloom o'ercast,
> They always must be with us, or we die.
>
>   [25-33]

There is no need to interpret this stanza in vague Neoplatonic terms, however, for it has a clear human psychological meaning. Keats's conception of beauty as an internalized essence is not distinct from, but is continuous with, his conception of its sensuous and erotic nature. By "beauty" Keats is basically referring to the experience of that first blissful harmony with our earliest love object and the subsequent internalization of that object as a "good" or idealized image. The specific associations in the first verse paragraph, the equation of beauty with a bower, with sleep and dreams, and, most significantly, with an "endless fountain" of drink "pouring" into us from above, all suggest the infant's experience at the breast. The second paragraph then describes how such an intense, erotically charged experience remains with us, becomes such a deep and integral part of us, that "whether there be shine, or gloom o'ercast, / They always must be with us, or we die." Why should one die if deprived of some "essences" of beauty? It seems to me that these lines make sense only psychologically, only if we understand "essences" as those internal, affectively cathectic objects that have become a part of the very structure of our selves and so, indeed, do determine our lives.

Murry implies a similar notion in nonpsychoanalytic language when he suggests that "beauty" is synonymous with "love" in Keats's mind. He refers to the letter (November 22, 1817) in which Keats avows, "I am certain of nothing but of the holiness of the Heart's affections—What the imagination seizes as Beauty must be truth—whether it existed before or not—for I have the same Idea of all our Passions as of Love; they are all in their sublime, creative of essential Beauty." Murry also quotes from a letter to Fanny: "I cannot conceive any beginning of such love as I have for you but Beauty." For Keats, then, the deep affections of the heart, Love and the Passions, are the source of Beauty, and thus one's experience of Beauty will feel to be the deepest, most intimate "truth" of one's personality. Endymion's quest for an ideal and essential Beauty in the form of the goddess, then, is essentially a quest to recover an ideal, infantile love. The "beauty" in *Ode on a Grecian Urn* reveals a similar idealized, regressive nature.[9] Endymion's ability finally to renounce the goddess reflects a developing maturity and integration in the poet's self, in his ability to love and to accept separateness and reality.

As Aileen Ward has pointed out, the birth of the poet's consciousness in *Endymion* is "linked with a dream of fulfilment in sexual love."[10] Through much of the poem, however, that love is of an exceedingly regressive, oral nature. Only a maturation in the love relationship can bring a real maturation in the poetic consciousness. The first image of Endymion recalls the Poet in Shelley's *Alastor*—a sensitive, solitary figure, "wan and pale," brooding alone, "A lurking trouble in his nether lip." He is isolated by his extreme suffering, and also by an innate superiority: "his garments

were a chieftain's king's." Keats also describes how "between / His
nervy knees there lay a boar-spear keen," which hints at a special
power that is specifically phallic and destructive. Endymion is cut
off not only from the common lot, but Keats also describes him as
cut off from reality, as out of touch with the world around him.
Endymion, he says, had "striven / To hide the cankering venom,
that had riven / His fainting recollection," but now

> His senses had swoon'd off: he did not heed
> The sudden silence, or the whispers low,
> Or the old eyes dissolving at his woe,
> Or anxious calls, or close of trembling palms,
> Or maiden's sigh, that grief itself embalms:
> But in the self-same fixed trance he kept,
> Like one who on the earth had never stept.
> Aye, even as dead still as a marble man,
> Frozen in that old tale Arabian.
>
> [396-405]

Endymion's condition as described here—the narcissistic isolation,
the inner division and deadness—indeed forms the central subject
of the poem. Keats is grappling with this narcissistic condition in
his poem and exploring its roots in an unresolved infantile love
relationship. By the end, Endymion is able to hear the maiden's
sigh of grief and to value his earthly home, thus being freed from
his paralyzing narcissism.

Immediately following the above description, Endymion's sister
Peona is introduced and, like the goddess, she is connected with
the ideal mother imago. She whispers to him "pantingly and
close" and leads him to a cradling bower, "Where nested was an
arbour, overwove / By many a summer's silent fingering; / To
whose cool bosom she was used to bring / Her playmates. . . ."
(431-34). In this maternal nest, Endymion drifts to sleep, a sleep he
calls "magic" for it is a "great key / To golden palaces, strange
minstrelsy, / Fountains grotesque, new trees, bespangled caves, /
Echoing grottos, full of tumbling waves / And moonlight; aye, to
all the mazy world / Of silvery enchantment!" (457-61). For Endymion, sleep is a regression, a magic return to the idealized maternal environment. This sleep, he feels, "renovates" him, much as
he feels the moon-goddess, who also comes upon him in his sleep,
is an "enchantment" that has "tortured" him with the promise of

"renewed life" (918-19). Endymion's account of this torturous enchantment occupies the remainder of Book 1.

The vision or dream first came upon him, he tells Peona, with the riveting sight of "the loveliest moon, that ever silver'd o'er / A shell for Neptune's goblet." For Keats, the moon is always associated with woman—"Thou wast the charm of woman, lovely Moon" (3: 169)—and he is troubled by the power she exerts over him: "'What is there in thee, Moon! that thou shouldst move / My heart so potently?'" (3: 142-43). Endymion's moon is so "passionately bright" that he feels his soul "commingling with her argent spheres." This feeling of intense communion and identification with the feminine moon heralds his vision of the goddess— "that completed form of all completeness." The goddess becomes the poet's all in all; she is a dream that he yet experiences as an overpowering reality, a subjective reality that comes to supersede any objective one. Endymion's description of erotic union with the goddess resembles comparable scenes in Shelley's poetry:

> —She took an airy range,
> And then, towards me, like a very maid,
> Came blushing, waning, willing, and afraid,
> And press'd me by the hand: Ah! 'twas too much;
> Methought I fainted at the charmed touch.
> . . . .
> I was distracted; madly did I kiss
> The wooing arms which held me, and did give
> My eyes at once to death: but 'twas to live,
> To take in draughts of life from the gold fount
> Of kind and passionate looks; to count, and count
> The moments, by some greedy help that seem'd
> A second self, that each might be redeem'd
> And plunder'd of its load of blessedness.
>
> [633-37, 653-60]

As Shelley's scenes of erotic union always end in dissolution and dissipation, so Endymion faints at contact with his goddess and feels that he is surrendering himself to a kind of death. The regressive content in the scene is unmistakable. Especially revealing is the poet's feeling of a "second self" greedily plundering the erotic delights. One can understand that second self as the poet's subliminal infantile self, hungrily engaging in greedy, illicit feelings toward the mother. The fantasy, however, is dangerous and cannot be sustained; the goddess disappears and the dream falls "into nothing." The poet projects his feelings of abandonment and betrayal onto the natural world, which now appears to him as dim and withdrawn and subtly sinister: "Away I wander'd—all the pleasant hues / Of heaven and earth had faded: deepest shades / Were deepest dungeons; heaths and sunny glades / Were full of pestilent light; . . ." (691-94).

Peona, like Keats himself, recognizes the unhealthiness of this obsessive dream. Out of pity, she refrains from scolding, "Shame / On this poor weakness!" (718). She does, however, inquire, "Then wherefore sully the entrusted gem / Of high and noble life with thoughts so sick?" (756-58). Endymion's reply, the defense of his passionate dream which follows, has generally been the focus of the critical controversy over the poem: "Wherein lies happiness? In that which becks / Our ready minds to fellowship divine, / A fellowship with essence; till we shine, / Full alchemiz'd, and free of space" (777-80). If we recall the very particular meaning which divine "essence" has for Keats at the beginning of the poem, this passage may seem less obscure than it does at first reading. A divine or beautiful essence, as we have seen, is connected in Keats's mind with the image of the ideal mother. That fellowship with essence and, more importantly, the divine "self-destroying" love that he goes on to describe express a longing for a regressive fusion with the ideal mother:

> There hangs by unseen film an orbed drop
> Of light, and that is love: its influence,
> Thrown in our eyes, genders a novel sense,
> At which we start and fret; till in the end,
> Melting into its radiance, we blend,
> Mingle, and so become a part of it,—
> Now with aught else can our souls interknit
> So wingedly: when we combine therewith,
> Life's self is nourish'd by its proper pith,
> And we are nurtured like a pelican brood.
> Aye, so delicious is the unsating food,
> That men, who might have tower'd in the van
> Of all the congregated world, . . .
> . . . .

Have been content to let occasion die,
Whilst they did sleep in love's elysium.

[806-25]

Not only do the images of melting, blending, and mingling suggest the regressive nature of this love, but so do the oral terms in which he describes it: the hanging "orbed drop" of love certainly suggests breast/milk, and the self is explicitly "nourished" and "nurtured" by this love. The love, however, is significantly "unsating" and renders one in a state of helpless passivity—the men "Have been content to let occasion die, / Whilst they did sleep in love's elysium." Endymion claims, though, that he would "rather be struck dumb, / Than speak against this ardent listlessness" (824-25). When critics latch on to the above passage as the key to some Neoplatonic meaning of the poem, they are neglecting that it is a defense of the poet's love for the goddess, and thus, when he finally renounces her, he is also renouncing the kind of love he espouses here. This criticism also applies to Murry's interpretation that the poem is about the "fusing" power of love. The poem really expresses the need to give up the desire for such a regressive, fusing love. Only by engaging in a more mature object love can the poet find real fulfillment.

Finally, the regressive and narcissistic nature of Endymion's love for the goddess is exposed once more at the end of Book 1. Ironically, while meaning further to defend his vision as more than an idle dream or solitary fantasy, Endymion tells Peona how he lately came upon a watery hollow, "when behold!" there he sees "The same bright face I tasted in my sleep, / Smiling in the clear well" (895-96). The face of the goddess is associated with the reflection of the poet's own face. As in "Alastor," the love for the ideal maiden or goddess is also a love for an ideal self.

In Book 2, before the poet descends into the deeper regions of the earth in search of his love, he appeals once more to the majestic moon to lessen the "tyranny" and "torment" of love, and to give him wings so that he might fly to his goddess. Almost as if the wish were granted, the poet suddenly experiences both the ecstasy and the terror of that regressive fusion for which he yearns:

I do think the bars
That kept my spirit in are burst—that I

Am sailing with thee through the dizzy sky!
. . . .
       When this thy chariot attains
Its airy goal, haply some bower veils
Those twilight eyes? Those eyes!—my spirit fails—
Dear goddess, help! or the wide-gaping air
Will gulph me—help!'

                                    [2: 186-89, 191-95]

As Shelley warns "Lift not the painted veil" for behind it lies a chasm "sightless and drear," so Endymion is terrified of "those twilight eyes" that he fantasizes behind his goddess's veil. Endymion, like Shelley, would prefer to keep his ideal woman veiled, for to meet her eyes means actually to confront the woman, to confront the mother whose eyes the infant self most likely experienced as dead, unseeing, unreflecting. The intense hunger and rage that experience initially provoked is evident in Endymion's fear that he is going to be "gulphed" and devoured. He projects his own hungry rage onto the mother and dreads a consuming annihilation.

Immediately following this fantasy, Endymion hears a voice commanding him to descend, to venture into "the hollow / The silent mysteries of earth." Much as the landscape in *Alastor* alternates between frozen wastelands and voluptuous bowers, so the subterranean landscape as described in the remainder of Book 2 reflects the same primitive ambivalence. The first region Endymion wanders through is a "dusky empire" of cold marble and sparkling gems, of "lines abrupt and angular," an environment that is essentially cold, silent, and petrified. He crosses a bridge "Athwart a flood of crystal" and feels his bosom grow "chilly and numb." The poet soon wearies of this deathly environment, and Keats describes how the poet sits down "before the maw / Of a wide outlet, fathomless and dim," and is visited by "shadows grim" and "thoughts of self" which are "crude and sore." The "journey homeward to habitual self," he says, is like "A mad-pursuing of the fog-born elf, / Whose flitting lantern, through rude nettle-briar / Cheats us into a swamp, into a fire, / Into the bosom of a hated thing" (276-80). The poet's journey into the maternal earth is also a journey into the self. The "dusky empire" reflects the murky, dissociated landscape of the poet's internal world of object relations. Thus, the cold and unresponsive, deathlike realm he has traversed only leads him back along a "crude and sore" path to a "hated" self.

As he sits "Desponding o'er the marble floor's cold thrill" (the tug between desire and repulsion again apparent), Endymion pleads with his goddess to "Deliver me from this rapacious deep!" (331). He then begins his journey back to the upper earth, and the environment suddenly switches from the cold and hateful to the ideal and luxurious. The poet comes upon the voluptuous bowers of Venus and Adonis. The erotic delights of this place are, as usual, specifically oral; Endymion exclaims over the rich and snowy cream, the blooming plums and manna. Venus eventually leads him to a mossy bower where he meets his goddess and the encounter inspires Keats to some effusive rhapsodizing:

> "O known Unknown! from whom my being sips
> Such darling essence, wherefore may I not
> Be ever in these arms? in this sweet spot
> Pillow my chin for ever? ever press
> These toying hands and kiss their smooth excess?
> Why not for ever and ever feel
> That breath about my eyes? Ah, thou wilt steal
> Away from me again, indeed, indeed—
> . . . .
> Those lips, O slippery blisses, twinkling eyes
> And by these tenderest, milky sovereignities—
> The tenderest, and by the nectar-wine
> The passion"—
>
> [739-47, 758-61]

The excesses and lack of judgment in the poetic style, the florid diction, the repetitive insistence and emotional overindulgence, reflect the immaturity of the vision itself. The greater restraint and concentration that come to characterize Keats's later style accompany the poet's increasing ability to surmount his obsession with an infantile fusing love and to integrate his ambivalently split internal relationships. In this passage, however, Endymion is so overcome by his ideal love, and particularly by her "milky sovereignities," that he is unable to connect or even finish his thoughts. He wishes only to "melt" into her and "entwine hoveringly." Finally he swoons, having "Drunken from pleasure's nipple" (868-69).

The goddess disappears once more and Endymion, again forlorn, feels, "Now I have tasted her sweet soul to the core / All other depths are shallow." Book 2 ends with his meeting two other unhappy lovers, Alpheus, the river-god, and the stream nymph, Aresthusa, and praying to his goddess to "assuage" these lovers' pains. He then looks up to find "the giant sea above his head;" his journey through the hollows of the earth being now complete.

Although Endymion is still obsessed with his goddess at the completion of this stage of his journey, his ability at the end to focus on an unhappy love besides his own, to recognize that he is not alone in his suffering, and indeed to pray to his goddess not for his own but for the happiness of others, suggests some progress in the poet's inner journey of self-integration and maturation. His experiences in Book 3 further prepare him to overcome his narcissistic maternal attachment and to love realistically. In his encounter with Glaucus, Endymion is again able to externalize and identify with suffering outside himself. Glaucus's history parallels Endymion's own. As a young man he too felt "distemper'd longings" and, in a fit of misery, threw himself into the sea to visit "The ceaseless wonders of this ocean-bed." Glaucus realizes that there is "no need to tell" Endymion of these mysteries of the maternal deep "for I see / That thou has been a witness" (393-94). As Endymion wandered through the earth's hollows, so Glaucus had pursued his elusive love Scylla through the ocean's depths.

The ambivalent nature of the woman's love is again apparent in Glaucus's story, for he is punished for his ideal love by the "cruel enchantress" Circe. In Ovid's version of the story, Glaucus rejects Circe's love, which thus allows the goddess a vengeful motive for her cruel behavior. In Keats's tale, however, Glaucus is merely a victim of the goddess's evil duplicity. She first comes to him in the guise of the ideal mother: "She took me like a child of suckling time, / And cradled me in roses" (3: 456-57). As usual, she vanishes, only to reappear as an "angry witch," a sadistic queen, "fierce, wan and tyrannizing" (508). Glaucus describes how "disgust and hate, / And terrors manifold divided me" (562-63). He feels his hand "upon a dead thing's face," which he discovers belongs to Scylla. All round him "Twas vast, and desolate, and icy cold" and he observes his limbs become "Gaunt, wither'd sapless, feeble, cramp'd and lame" (638). Glaucus believes he is being punished for having succumbed to Circe's original charms, to that idyllic maternal love that she first promised. When describing that moment to Endymion, he tries to defend himself: "Who could resist? Who in this universe? / She did so breathe ambrosia; so immerse / My fine existence in a golden clime" (452-54). Glaucus thus senses that in his love for the goddess there is something illicit, punishable. He is indeed punished for the destructive rage that lurks in his love for the mother. Endymion, he believes, is the "restoring chance" that is going to "quell / One half of the witch in me" (644-45).

When Endymion hears that he has been decreed to break the spell over Glaucus, he is "overjoy'd" and cries, "We are twin brothers in this destiny!" (712). He frees Glaucus and also revives the captive drowned lovers of centuries past. A celebration ensues in which Venus promises Endymion a future reunion with his goddess and the book ends with Endymion crying, "I die—I hear her voice—I feel my wing"—as he feels himself borne away in the "cradling arms" of the Nereids towards "a crystal bower far away." Endymion is obviously still self-destructively attached to the image of the ideal mother. The fantasy he has enjoyed in the course of Book 3, however, the identification and complicity with the father figure Glaucus, helps bolster him for the future severence of that maternal attachment.

In the seven-month period during which Keats worked on *Endymion*, his own life, as Ward discusses it, took some important emotional turns. The autumn of 1817, prior to the writing of Book 4, was especially eventful. His brother Tom fell ill, betraying the first ominous signs of consumption, and Keats himself contracted a venereal disease, probably syphilis, which no doubt affected him deeply. He was, furthermore, becoming increasingly disillusioned with Hunt and with himself and discouraged with his own poetry.[11] Ward believes that these disillusionments of the autumn profoundly altered the naive idealism with which he had begun the poem and can thus help account for the "astonishing inversion" that takes place in the legend in Book 4. Doubtless these events did influence Keats's writing; nevertheless, one need not look outside the poem in order to understand the ending. From the beginning, Endymion's obsessive, idealized love for the goddess has been a part of an obsessive yearning for a self-destructive fusing love. By immersing himself in the "deep mysteries" of earth and sea, by venturing through hidden and forbidden territory in Books 2 and 3, he finally becomes confident and autonomous enough by Book 4 to relinquish that obsession and love realistically.

Finding himself back on the earth, on the soil of his native England at the beginning of Book 4, Endymion cries, "Ah, woe is me! that I should fondly part / From my dear native land!" (30-31). While experiencing a new-found gratitude for even "one short hour / Of native air," Endymion overhears a lonely lament that curiously echoes his own late grief:

> "Is no one near to help me? No fair dawn
> Of life from charitable voice? No sweet saying
> To set my dull and sadden'd spirit playing?
> No hand to toy with mine? No lips so sweet
> That I may worship them? No eyelids meet
> To twinkle on my bosom? No one dies
> Before me, till from these enslaving eyes
> Redemption sparkles!—I am sad and lost."
>
> [44-51]

The voice belongs to an Indian maiden with whom Endymion feels a "kindred pain," a pain that becomes a love as intense as that for his goddess. Endymion now feels guilty and confused; his love for the maid seems at first a betrayal of his goddess. He feels "for both my love is so immense, / I feel my heart is cut for them in twain," and he questions, "Why am I not as are the dead, / Since to a woe like this I have been led / Through the dark earth, and through the wondrous sea?" (89-91). But it is precisely to this woe, to the painful acceptance of aloneness and the impossibility of recovering an infantile fusion with the mother, that his journeys have significantly led him. Endymion's feeling of gratitude toward the earth/mother at the opening of Book 4 demonstrates an increasing maturity, and his ability to feel compassion and love for the maiden finally signifies a move out of narcissistic isolation and into real human relations. Although Endymion still feels a strong passion for the goddess, the guilt and confusion he now experiences over that passion are a natural product of his growth. The poet comes to integrate the pain of separateness and loss, of frustration and anger, into his feelings of love. The ability to accept and mourn the loss of the idealized mother imago and to experience

depressed feelings of anger and guilt over that loss marks a maturation in the personality, in its capacity to experience real object
love. Endymion's love for the earthly maiden is itself an acceptance
of loss and sorrow. Keats has the Indian maiden sing a long and
rueful roundelay—a Song of Sorrow—which so moves Endymion
with its sweet sadness that he feels, "I must be thy sad servant
evermore." The poet's acceptance of sorrow is thus one with his
newborn capacity to experience human love.

Endymion's trials, however, are not yet over. His goddess, "his
delicious lady," appears to him again, but when he reaches out to
slake his passion, she once more melts away. Endymion's ambivalent ties to the mother still prevent him from completely embracing
the maiden, from fully engaging in real object love. He cries,
"Would I were whole in love!" His lack of wholeness in love betrays the lack of wholeness in self: "What is this soul then?" he
moans, "Whence came it? It does not seem my own, and I / Have
no self-passion or identity" (474-76). The passage that then follows
again emphasizes the ambivalence at the root of the poet's inner
division and confusion. Endymion looks up to see "The moon put
forth a little diamond peak," which suggests a phallic destructiveness in the mother image, and that image heralds the devastating
fantasy that follows. When Endymion turns to his maiden,

> Despair! despair!
> He saw her body fading gaunt and spare
> In the cold moonshine, Straight he seiz'd her wrist;
> It melted from his grasp: her hand he kiss'd,
> And, horror! kiss'd his own—he was alone.
>
> [506-10]

The poet is horrified not simply by the maiden's disappearance
but by his having kissed his own hand, by the narcissistic nature
of his own love. Unlike Lycius, who is pleased to look into Lamia's
eyes only to see himself "mirror'd small in paradise," Endymion's
horror bespeaks a desire to move beyond such a narcissistic and
self-destroying love. He is finally ready to relinquish a love for an
ideal mother/self and to accept a more limited but real love for
another human being. Endymion's revelations in the Cave of
Quietude articulate this readiness.

The poet enters the cave "Made for the soul to wander in and trace / Its own existence," where the soul can uncover its "buried griefs," and he emerges with a newly found appreciation and acceptance of reality. He finds his Indian maiden waiting for him upon his return and he exclaims,

> ... now I see
> The grass; I feel the solid ground—
> ... let us fare
> On forest fruits and never, never go
> Among the abodes of mortals here below,
> Or be by phantoms duped
>
> [621-29]

He then explains,

> I have clung
> To nothing, lov'd a nothing, nothing seen
> Or felt but a great dream! O I have been
> Presumptuous against love, against the sky,
> Against all elements, against the tie
> Of mortals each to each, ...
> . . . .
> My sweetest Indian, here,
> Here will I kneel, for thou redeemed hast
> My life from too thin breathing: gone and past
> Are cloudy phantasms. Caverns lone, farewell!
> And air of visions, and the monstrous swell
> Of visionary seas! ...
> . . . .
> My Indian bliss!
> My river-lily bud! one human kiss!
> One sigh of real breath—one gentle squeeze,
> Warm as a dove's nest among summer trees,
> And warm with dew as ooze from living blood!
>
> [636-43, 648-53, 663-67]

Endymion has one more test, however, to endure. The maiden, by some mysterious decree, has been forbidden to him. The poet is thus forced to experience loss and aloneness before achieving his fulfillment. He resolves to leave the maiden and live as a hermit. Alone once more, he watches an autumnal sunset and is deeply moved by its melancholy beauty. He realizes that the bliss in love he had formerly sought, because devoid of the reality of separateness and loss, has merely been an empty fantasy "Of flowers, garlands, love-knots, silly posies." The understanding and acceptance of reality and of self which Endymion has at last gained gives him the strength to assert himself and heroically to affirm the value of life and of real love. Upon meeting the maiden one last time, he renounces a morbid hermetic existence and defies the fateful decree by grasping the maiden's hand and declaring, "I would have command, / If it were heaven's will, on our sad fate" (974-75). At this the maiden exclaims, "And so thou shalt!" and miraculously she is transformed into the golden-haired goddess. In the final lines of the poem, she explains to Endymion that he has been "Spiritualized" by some "unlook'd for change" in the course of his adventures. This suggests, as Ward observes, that the maid's transformation is less a mere fairy-tale device than a symbolic expression of a psychological transformation. Ward claims that when Endymion "finally realizes that to renounce the maid is to deny life itself, he is rewarded by the maid's transformation into the goddess; that is, real love, when accepted for the good it contains, leads to the fulfillment Endymion has sought all along."[12] Endymion has at last become whole in love, and the maiden's transformation symbolizes that wholeness. The goddess and the maiden have become one; Endymion has made whole the object of his love. The maiden has become the goddess, but, as Ward points out, the goddess herself has been humanized; for by yielding to a mortal lover, she has defied the decree of fate which had doomed her to eternal chastity.

Endymion finally succeeds in his struggle to give the woman wholeness and reality. For Keats, however, the struggle remained an ever-present one, for he continually reenacts it in his poetry. He repeatedly had to resist a pull toward a regressive, fusing love and toward idealized fantasies of the mother and the self. The tension is the source of the enmity he constructs between the dreamer and the poet. The dreamer is the narcissist, hopelessly fixated on his own idealizations and fantasies, whereas the poet speaks always for relationship with the real world outside the self. *The Fall of Hyperion*, the unfinished poem that Keats labored over in the final months of his life, explicitly dramatizes this struggle and again reveals its roots in an archaic maternal ambivalence.

THE FALL OF HYPERION:
CONFRONTING THE MOTHER
AND A TRAGIC REALITY

Like Shelley's *Triumph of Life*, Keats's *Fall* has its structural
source in Dante's *Purgatorio*. Dissatisfied with what he considered
the artificiality of the Miltonic mode of *Hyperion*, Keats decided
to recast his epic about the fall of the Titans into a more personal
and allegorical form. As he felt compelled to deal more freely and
directly with internal psychological realities, Dante indeed provided the more suitable model. In *The Fall*, Keats, like Shelley in
The Triumph, casts himself as a poet undergoing a purgatorial
experience. Also as with Shelley's *Triumph*, the manuscript was
abandoned before completion. The similarities between the two
poems, however, do not stop there. Both are concerned with a
dream, with a subjective vision that centers on the figure of a
powerful, mythical woman. Although it is impossible to say how
either poem might have been revised and finished had the poets
continued to live, it is possible to distinguish, even in the fragmented forms of the poems, two very different directions in the
treatment of a similar crisis.

Before launching into the story of *The Fall*, Keats begins with a
discussion of dreams. He draws a distinction between the dreams
of the poet and those of the fanatic and the savage:

> Fanatics have their dreams, wherewith they weave
> A paradise for a sect; the savage too
> From forth the loftiest fashion of his sleep
> Guesses at Heaven; pity these have not
> Trac'd upon vellum or wild Indian leaf
> The shadows of melodious utterance.
> But bare of laurel they live, dream, and die;
> For Poesy alone can tell her dreams,
> With the fine spell of words alone can save
> Imagination from the sable charm
> And dumb enchantment.
>
> > [1-10]

The stanza goes on to explain that since everyone has dreams,
everyone is a potential poet. Whether the dream which he is about
to relate, however, "Be a poet's or fanatic's" will be known only

"when this warm scribe my hand is in the grave." Keats significantly chooses the fanatic and the savage with whom to compare the poet, for it is precisely the obsessive and primitive qualities of his dream which would conceivably disturb him. "The Fall" deals directly with the poet's obsessive feelings and primitive, infantile conflicts concerning the mother, and thus Keats had reason to question his control or mastery of the material.

The tale opens with an Edenic scene, with images of an ideal maternal environment. The poet finds himself surrounded by lush trees and fountains, in "an arbour with a drooping roof / Of trellis vines." The oral/breast images are rampant. The poet describes how "on a mount / Of moss, was spread a feast of summer fruits" (28-29). There "was more plenty than the fabled horn / Thrice emptied could pour forth" (35-36), and the poet feels an "appetite / More yearning than on Earth I ever felt / Growing within, I ate deliciously" (37-40). After eating, the poet stresses his consequent thirst and describes a "cool vessel of transparent juice" from which he deeply drinks. "That full draught," he asserts, "is parent of my theme." As usual in Keats's poetry, the poet falls into a "cloudy swoon" immediately after drinking. That swoon, or regressive sleep, results in the visionary adventures that follow, adventures that take their form and temper from the ambivalence that lies behind that initial oral experience.

When the poet first awakens from his swoon, he finds himself deprived of the voluptuous fruits of the former setting: "the fair trees were gone, / The mossy mound and arbour were no more" (59-60). He looks instead upon "the carved sides / Of an old sanctuary with roof august," an "eternal domed Monument." This marble environment, however, is still associated with the mother; not only is the dome suggestive of the breast, but it is also covered with feminine trappings—"strange vessels and large draperies," robes and white linen, "Girdles, and chains, and holy jewelries." The scene recalls that "dusky empire" of cold marble and hard gems which Endymion encounters in the lower regions of the earth—a maternal environment that is petrified, cold, and indifferent. Like Endymion, the poet in *The Fall* is preparing to confront his ambivalent feelings and to relinquish his narcissistic fantasies concerning the mother by undergoing a series of tests. He is first challenged by a voice from the marble altar which threatens him with the following command:

If thou canst not ascend
These steps, die on that marble where thou art.
Thy flesh, near cousin to the common dust,
Will parch for lack of nutriment—thy bones
Will wither in few years, and vanish so
That not the quickest eye could find a grain
Of what thou now art on that pavement cold.

[107-13]

The poet is terrified by what seems a "prodigious" task. He is struck by a "palsied chill" that ascends from the marble floor up through his limbs, a paralyzing cold and "numbness" which "Grew stifling, suffocating, at the heart" (130). The poet is experiencing the same deadly chill Endymion suffers during his descent into mother/self, "into the bosom of a hated thing." The poet's ability simply to face and experience these cold and hateful feelings, however, is itself a first step toward self-integration and maturity. Thus, as his foot touches the lowest stair, he feels a surge of renewed life and is able to mount the ladder to the veiled and "holy Power" before him. The "veiled shadow" indeed tells the poet that he has been saved precisely because he was able to endure those deathlike feelings: "—'Thou has felt / What 'tis to die and live again before / Thy fated hour, that thou hadst power to do so / Is thy own safety; . . .'" (141-44). She informs him further that "None can usurp this height . . . / But those to whom the miseries of the world / Are misery, and will not let them rest" (147-49). This puzzles the poet, for he is aware that "thousands in the world" love and suffer and "feel the giant agony of the world" while he alone is on the steps. The voice replies with a withering rebuke; the poet is informed that he is different from, indeed "less" than, the others:

"Those whom thou spak'st of are no vision'ries,"
Rejoin'd that voice—"They are no dreamers weak,
They seek no wonder but the human face;
No music but a happy-noted voice—
They come not here, they have no thought to come—
And thou are here, for thou art less than they—
What benefit canst thou, or all thy tribe,
To the great world? Thou art a dreaming thing,
A fever of thyself—think of the Earth;

[161-69]

The poet is accused of the same unhealthy, culpable behavior as Endymion; he is condemned for his narcissistic idealism. By chasing after his own fantasies and idealizations, he is betraying both the real world—the Earth, his true "home"—and humankind. Keats reveals an awareness of the self-destructive, masochistic nature of this narcissistic idealism. "Only the dreamer venoms all his days, / Bearing more woe than all his sins deserve." That the dreamer is guilty of being unable to experience "The pain alone; the joy alone; distinct," suggests that the *Ode on Melancholy*, which is about the very convergence of the two, is an expression of the dreamer rather than the poet. When Keats tells us in the *Ode* that "in the very temple of delight / Veil'd Melancholy has her sovran shrine," when he urges the melancholic to go to nature to "glut" his sorrow, to "feed deep" upon the "peerless eyes" of his angry mistress, and to "burst Joy's grape" so that he might "taste the sadness of her might," he is again revealing, indeed revelling in, a masochistic attachment to the mother.[13] As A. E. Rodway has pointed out, the anguish in the *Ode* is a "desired anguish."[14] In *The Fall*, however, Keats displays a critical awareness of his masochistic inclinations. The true poet, he realizes, does not indulge in his own pain and sorrow, he does not look to be hung among Melancholy's "cloudy tropies"; contrarily, he urges health, he is "A humanist, a physician to all men." The poet is the "sheer opposite" of the dreamer: "The one pours out a balm upon the World, / The other vexes it" (201-2). With this realization, the poet in *The Fall* is at last fully ready to confront the mother and his ambivalent feelings toward her. He asks the "Majestic shadow" to reveal herself to him.

The goddess introduces herself as Moneta, "Sole Priestess of this desolation." The mother figure thus again reigns over and is responsible for the barren, forsaken condition. As Walter Jackson Bate points out, Moneta is both "mother of the muses" and also, as the Latin name suggests, an "admonisher."[15] The poet likens the softness of her words to those of a mother's while also betraying his lingering ambivalence and fear: "And yet I had a terror of her robes, / And chiefly of the veils, that from her brow / Hung pale, and curtain'd her in mysteries, / That made my heart too small to hold its blood" (251-54). Moneta then unveils herself, and the passage is one of the most powerful and justly celebrated moments in all of Keats's poetry. Whereas Endymion, upon fantasizing his goddess's eyes behind her veils, dissolves in a terror of being "gulphed" and annihilated, the poet in *The Fall* has acquired the strength and maturity not only to face and contemplate the mother's deathly, unseeing eyes but to find in them benignancy and peace.

> This saw that Goddess, and with sacred hand
> Parted the veils. Then saw I a wan face,
> Not pin'd by human sorrows, but bright-blanch'd
> By an immortal sickness which kills not;
> It works a constant change, which happy death
> Can put no end to; deathwards progressing
> To no death was that visage; it had past
> The lily and the snow; and beyond these
> I must not think now, though I saw that face—
> But for her eyes I should have fled away.
> They held me back, with a benignant light,
> Soft mitigated by divinest lids
> Half-closed, and visionless entire they seem'd
> Of all external things;—they saw me not,
> But in blank splendour, beam'd like the mild moon,
> Who comforts those she sees not, . . .
>
> [255-70]

The moon is no longer associated with a tantalizing ideal goddess as in *Endymion*. The poet of *The Fall* is able to look in the moon/mother's face and see death as well as love and compassion. The moon, as the poet affirms later, is "a whole moon." The mother is no longer split between the ideal and the treacherous. By confronting the mother in her separate, "indifferent" otherness, by accepting his deepest feelings of enraged loss and sorrow, the poet is at last able to concentrate his experiences into a vision of a whole reality that includes both love and loss. Moneta's face is the symbolic expression of that vision. Ward's claim that the sightless and compassionate face is "the face of his dead mother, shrouded for her coffin," need not reduce the meaning and resonance of the passage. The interpretation does not depend on the literal fact of the mother's death. The face is also that of a mother experienced by the infant self as dead and unseeing, and that crucial experience informs the personality and the poetry at its deepest level. Ward notes that Yeats (whose personality and poetry bare many similarities with Keats's) believed that the image of Moneta's face was the "'one scene, one adventure, one picture' . . . which 'if he could brood over it his life long, would bring him in the end to an understanding of all his experience'" (p. 340). F. R. Leavis also points to the Moneta passage as one of Keats's most profound achievements. The passage, he says, demonstrates an ability to experience pain and loss as objects, as facts. The "tragic impersonality" of the vision, he adds, is closely related to the superb *Ode to Autumn*.[16] Keats's finest poetry indeed reflects a hard-won resolution of his earliest ambivalent love relationship. The integration of his own loving and destructive feelings toward the mother imago, and his acceptance of her as a whole reality, neither solely loving or destructive, enables him to move beyond a narcissistic subjectivism in his poetry and to render a richer, more complex experience of reality.

The remainder of *The Fall* returns to the theme of the fallen Titans and is largely a reworking of the first *Hyperion*. The poem was abandoned perhaps because the source of its creative energy, its motivating conflict, lies in the poet's confrontation with Moneta, and thus when Keats completed that passage, he felt no compelling need to continue. The mythical theme, however, is nonetheless related to the personal one. Keats's fascination with the ruined gods, with the fall of the Titans from a state of grace and omnipotence, reflects his preoccupation with the loss of narcissistic omnipotence. The force behind Keats's story of *The Fall* is his need to come to terms with the impossibility of regaining an idealized oneness or identification with the all-powerful mother. With the recognition and acceptance of the pain and loss comes the birth of compassion, and that is the real story that *The Fall* chronicles. The most prominent and powerful images in the poem all portray a woman's compassion — Moneta's face, Saturn with his bowed head, "listening to the Earth / His ancient mother, for some comfort yet" (325-26), the goddess with hand "pressed upon that aching spot / Where beats the human heart, as if just there, / Though an immortal, she felt cruel pain" (344-46), and the one scene that bores in upon the poet's consciousness with the force of an epiphany:

> . . . A long awful time
> I look'd upon them: still they were the same;
> The frozen God still bending to the earth,

> And the sad Goddess weeping at his feet,
> Moneta silent.

[384-88]

With the personal integration that *The Fall* achieves comes a simultaneous sharpening of perception and deepening comprehension of external reality. The very style of the poem reflects this integrity. The concentrated synthesis of image and thought, the concreteness and restraint, the steady focus on the object, what Leavis calls "a firm grasp of actuality in the field of tragic experience," all reflect the integration of the poet's internal world of object relations.[17]

Keats's finest odes display a similar integration of the narcissistic loss into a whole vision of self and reality. In *Ode to a Nightingale*, for instance, the poet identifies his deep feelings of abandonment and loss, beautifully imaged in the portrait of Ruth, as part of a historical human identity. Thus it is that one word, "Forlorn," which, in the final stanza, tolls the poet back from his regressive desire to escape with the nightingale to the deepest truth of his personality, to his "sole self," to reality. *To Autumn* realizes a similar success in its integration of the regressive, feminine, and melancholic feelings with assertive, masculine, and affirmative ones, and in its balanced harmony of life and death images.[18] This vision of an integrated whole reality is the achievement of a personality that has integrated its feelings of loss and rage and thereby made itself whole. In his best work, Keats the poet triumphs over Keats the dreamer. The dreamer's tendency to retreat into a static and timeless fantasy world of ideal self-images and object images is defeated by the poet's affirmation of the material world of fact and process, by his acceptance of the pain, change, and loss that inevitably accompany growth.

·3·

COLERIDGE

CHRISTABEL:
THE DRAMA OF AMBIVALENCE

Introduction

Coleridge's poetry has inspired much psychoemotional and psychosexual criticism. In order to explain the emotional power of such dreamlike and irrational poems as *Christabel, The Rime of the Ancient Mariner,* and *Kubla Khan,* critics have been forced to look beyond the immediate supernatural surface to underlying psychological dimensions. The sexual currents in Coleridge's poetry, furthermore, are obvious enough to have excited attention. G. Wilson Knight, for instance, has commented on the "strangely feminine" character in the first part of *Christabel* and he claims that the poem generally expresses "fear of some nameless obscenity."[1] Several critics have connected this "nameless" evil presence in *Christabel* with a specifically sexual evil. Roy Basler, for instance, says that the poem is about the dark "inscrutable power of sexual necessity." He talks about a homosexual relationship between Christabel and Geraldine and about the "transforming" power of sex in the poem. He believes that the poem intended to trace a transformation in the character of the evil Geraldine by means of her "sexual contact" with the good and innocent Christabel.[2] Using a similar psychosexual approach, however, Gerald Enscoe comes to just the opposite conclusion. He claims that it is Christabel who is meant to be rescued and transformed; through a sexual awakening with an essentially benevolent Geraldine, Christabel is saved from a blind and deathlike state of innocence. Enscoe admits, however, the ambiguity in Coleridge's attitude, due to the ambivalent treatment of the Geraldine-Christabel relationship.[3]

This problem of ambivalence is what all interpretations of *Christabel*, psychosexual and other, eventually must confront. Even those critics who see in the poem a Gothic tale of terror and who ascribe to it a religious or purely moral meaning are faced with the complex indeterminateness of the "good" and "bad" characters in the poem (an indeterminateness to which Basler's and Enscoe's contradictory interpretations attest). The critics all agree that *Christabel* is concerned with the problem of good and evil and that it dramatizes a moral struggle. The unresolved and complex nature of that struggle, however, is due to its being psychologically rooted in an unresolved ambivalent love relationship. Virginia Radley in "Christabel" claims that the ambivalent love relationship is precisely what the poem is all about. Radley points to the ambivalence in all of the several love relations in the poem: Christabel with Geraldine, Leoline with Christabel, and Leoline with Lord Roland. She suggests a psychological source for the poem in the nightmares Coleridge recorded in the *Notebooks*. In one dream he describes a woman of darkness who is wrenching at his right eye, and, in another, of a "frightful pale woman" whose breath was lethal. Radley, however, does not explore the psychic basis of Coleridge's ambivalent attitude. She stops with the suggestion that *Christabel* portrays ambivalent feelings toward the loved one as "the natural condition of intense love." Radley's study, as she admits herself, is only a beginning; it indicates an important direction for further critical study. She describes the problem but does not analyze its psychic and emotional origins. In a review of the research on the poem, Thomas Raysor and Max Schulz complain that the psychological approaches of Radley and others "do not explain why Coleridge should be so preoccupied presumably with ambivalent love."[4] The explanation need not be culled from Coleridge's biography but can be found within the poetry itself.

In brief, Coleridge's ambivalence stems from his unresolved

attachment to the mother imago. Coleridge's poetry everywhere projects a personality fixated on an infantile oral relationship with the mother. Breast and oral images are abundant, and in his pre-occupation with sleep, Coleridge betrays both an intense desire for and a terror of a self-annihilating regressive fusion. The passivity and "indolence" that he so often chastises himself for in the poetry and the letters also suggest a struggle to resist a regressive tendency. Even his criticism and metaphysics reflect the unresolved nature of his internal object relations. His major critical and philosophical theories all revolve around the concept of wholeness, of unity or identification with an omnipotent, all-encompassing One. The wish underlying his theories is always to bridge the gap between the inner self and external Nature. Coleridge's passion for wholeness and unity arises out of his need to overcome an internal division, to mend a flaw or fracture in his internal relation with the mother imago. William Walsh puts it well when he describes Coleridge as possessing an "appetite for unity."[5] The hunger amounts to a preoccupation that, Walsh believes, has emotional and compensatory motives. The most intimate kind of unity, he explains, is identity—the coherent structure of the self. Coleridge's repeated stress on universal unity and organic harmony is thus also part of a personal need to establish an inner coherency and wholeness. As Kohut and others have shown, a coherent self-structure is built up through the internalization and integration of our earliest object relations.

The flaw in Coleridge's relationship with the mother imago is evident in the severely split images of women which appear throughout his poetry. Not only do the female images in *Christabel* alternate between the saving angel and the treacherous vampire, but *The Ancient Mariner* also splits a powerful female presence into an ideal and benevolent Mary Queen on the one hand, and the Nightmare Death-in-Life on the other. The "savage" and "holy" nature of the erotic landscape of *Kubla Khan* reflects the same ambivalence. The narcissistic personality traits that accompany this primitive ambivalence—the idealized self and mother fantasies and the underlying sense of a fragmented, unloved, and unformed self—are also characteristic of Coleridge's work. His poetry, however, unlike that of Shelley or Keats, is deeply shaded by feelings of guilt. His ability to experience depression, to feel responsibility for his enraged, destructive feelings, and to mourn the loss of his "good" objects, finally reflects a more mature, integrated ego than his severe ambivalence might at first suggest.

Several critics have written specifically about the decisive psychological role of the mother in Coleridge's poetry. J. Garth Ware, for instance, in "Coleridge's Great Poems Reflecting the Mother Image," claims that the good-bad omnipotent mother fantasy dominates Coleridge's three major poems. Ware believes that Coleridge projected his painful aggressive feelings onto the mother and consequently remained fixated on the phallic woman throughout his life. Coleridge, he claims, "never grew up." Eugene Sloane, in his study of *Kubla Khan*, also emphasizes the importance of the mother and of the phallic woman in the poetry. Although his interpretation of *Kubla Khan* as an "elaborate development of a birth dream" is not completely convincing, he does give an illuminating discussion of the specific images—all the dark enclosed places, the caves and caverns, the domes, and the sinuous rivers and spirals—in relation to the mother's body. He points to the image of the snake as symbolic of the preoedipal phallic mother. Earth goddesses, he explains, have historically been associated with snakes, snakes that often possess ambivalent and vampiric characteristics.[6]

In a psychoanalytic study of *The Ancient Mariner*, David Beres claims, like Sloane, that Coleridge was "a man who remained in his relationships to persons a never-satisfied, ever-demanding infant." He, too, discusses the prominence of the good-bad omnipotent mother fantasy in the poetry, and he also sees evidence of this split in Coleridge's real relations with woman. Coleridge saw Mrs. Evans, he believes, as an idealized, all-good mother, and his mother-in-law, Mrs. Fricker, as the bad and hated mother. Beres claims that the albatross in *The Ancient Mariner* represents the ambivalently loved mother. The albatross is first introduced with comments about food, and, like the mother, it is a source of protection and plenty. The mariner's shooting of the albatross is similar to Christabel's killing her mother in childbirth; both reflect Coleridge's destruction of his mother in his unconscious mind. The mariner's parching thirst following the killing of the albatross, the oral deprivation, is the logical punishment following the mother's murder. Finally, by blessing the snakes, representative of the phallic mother, the mariner gains absolution by accepting what was rejected. His reward is again imaged in oral terms—in the quenching of his thirst by the rains.[7]

Finally, Wormhoudt also analyzes Coleridge's poetry, and *Christabel* in particular, in terms of the mother-child relationship. Wormhoudt sees this relationship as characterized primarily by a psychic masochism. He quotes the lines from Crashaw's *Tears of St. Teresa*—"since 'tis not to be had at home / She'd travel to a martyrdom"—lines that Coleridge claimed were "ever present to the second part of *Christabel*—if, indeed, by some subtle process of mind they did not suggest the first thought of the entire poem." Wormhoudt thus maintains that the persecutor-martyr relationship is at the base of the mother-child relationship in the poem. Coleridge projects himself into the character of Christabel, he explains, disguising himself by the change in sex. The bulk of Wormhoudt's analysis focuses on the bad mother images in the poem and on the "negative oedipal relationship" between Christabel and her father. He sees the oedipal pattern as a defense against the more primary oral masochistic pattern. Too often, however, Wormhoudt forces the poem to conform to his theoretical structures, and his interpretations are not always substantiated by actual evidence within the poem itself (there is no evidence, for instance, of the "defensive" nature of the oedipal pattern he sees and of his general equation of words with milk in the poem).[8] The danger of reducing or stretching the poetry to fit preconceived patterns is, of course, a danger inherent in all criticism. Unfortunately, psychoanalytic criticism in the past has proved itself to be particularly susceptible. D. W. Harding makes this complaint about Beres's analysis of *The Ancient Mariner*. Harding argues that Beres does not pay close enough attention to the images themselves.[9] I believe, however, that one can examine the images closely and, in so doing, discover the psychic patterns that determine those images.

As Radley points out, the entire imagistic pattern of *Christabel* is structured on ambivalence. Before we investigate the poem's particular images, it is helpful to look at a short lyric published with *Christabel—The Pains of Sleep*. Coleridge begins the poem by discussing his preparations for sleep. It has not been his habit, he says, to kneel and pray,

> But silently, by slow degrees,
> My spirit I to Love compose

> In humble trust mine eye-lids close,
> With reverential resignation,
> No wish conceived, no thought exprest,
> Only a sense of supplication;

The poet, in other words, associates sleep with the abandonment of the self to a kind of Love—a Love that requires that he resign himself in reverence and supplication. Coleridge concludes the first stanza with the wishful declaration that though he is "weak," he is "yet not unblest / Since in me, round me, every where / Eternal Strength and Wisdom are."

The second verse paragraph, though, immediately belies this confidence as Coleridge's ambivalence becomes manifest:

> But yester-night I prayed aloud
> In anguish and in agony,
> Up starting from the fiendish crowd
> Of shapes and thoughts that tortured me:
> A lurid light, a trampling throng,
> Sense of intolerable wrong,
> And whom I scorned, those only strong!
> Thirst of revenge, the powerless will
> Still baffled, and yet burning still!
> Desire with loathing strangely mixed
> On wild and hateful objects fixed.
> Fantastic passions! maddening brawl!
> And shame and terror over all!
> Deeds to be hid which were not hid,
> Which all confused I could not know
> Whether I suffered, or I did:
> For all seemed guilt, remorse or woe,
> My own or others still the same
> Life-stifling fear, soul-stifling shame.

As in Shelley's *Triumph of Life*, the poet's nightmarish terror assumes the form of a "fiendish" and "trampling" crowd. The image also occurs in *Dejection: An Ode* when, in the seventh stanza, the poet describes a "rushing crowd" and the "groans of trampled men, with smarting wounds" as they "shudder with the cold." The overpowering upsurge of enraged and terrifying feelings that this trampling image projects is given still another dimension in Coleridge's poetry. Whereas in Shelley's *Triumph* the image is connected solely with the poet's feeling of being victimized, of being helplessly overcome by a hostile external power, in Coleridge's poem the trampling throng is connected with the poet's own "Sense of intolerable wrong." The poem expresses less self-pity than it does "shame," "guilt," "remorse," and "woe." Shelley's poet accuses a treacherously feminine Life of thwarting and stifling him; Coleridge acknowledges that he is being stifled by his own fear and shame. He intuitively recognizes the profound ambivalence at the source of this disturbed condition: "Desire with loathing strangely mixed / On wild and hateful objects fixed." The ambivalent fixation on "wild" and "hateful" objects relates specifically, as we shall see, to the child's ambivalent attachment to the mother.

In the third and final stanza, the poet describes how after two more nights of cursed sleep, he awoke on the third night

> O'ercome with sufferings strange and wild,
> I wept as I had been a child;
> And having thus by tears subdued
> My anguish to a milder mood,
> Such punishments, I said, were due
> To natures deepliest stained with sin, —

The adjectives "strange and wild" associate the sufferings here with the "wild" objects that inspire the "strangely mixed" desire with loathing. This painful ambivalence and suffering is specifically related to a child's pain and suffering: "I wept as I had been a child." The connection is made even more explicit in *Dejection* when, immediately following the poet's description of the trampling crowds, he tells the following tale:

> A tale of less affright,
> And tempered with delight,
> As Otway's self had framed the tender lay, —
> Tis of a little child
> Upon a lonesome wild,
> Not far from home, but she hath lost her way:
> And now moans low in bitter grief and fear,
> And now screams loud, and hopes to make her mother hear.

The lost and abandoned child (the image alludes to Wordsworth's "Lucy" poems) full of "bitter grief and fear" who screams loudly in hopes of making her mother hear is thus closely associated with the wild and desperate rushing crowds, with the terror and bitter groans of the trampled men which come before. The child's intense feelings of loss, of bitterness and anger toward the mother fill her with an overwhelming shame as well as a terror of being punished and destroyed by her own destructive feelings.

In the final lines of *The Pains of Sleep*, Coleridge bewails the tyrannical and compulsive nature of this ambivalent fixation and ultimately he attempts to defend himself by a sudden and complete denial:

> For aye entempesting anew
> The unfathomable hell within,
> The horror of their deeds to view,
> To know and loath, yet wish and do!
> Such griefs with such men well agree,
> But wherefore, wherefore fall on me?
> To be beloved is all I need,
> And whom I love, I love indeed.

He is right that "To be beloved is all I need," but whom he loves he also hates. This defensive denial is even more apparent in an earlier version of the stanza: "But I—Oh, wherefore this on me? / Frail is my soul, yea, strengthless wholly, / Unequal, restless, melancholy. / But free from Hate and sensual Folly."

Coleridge is tormented precisely because he is *not* "free from Hate and sensual Folly." He is indeed enslaved by the obsessive-compulsive nature of his ambivalence, and this enslavement is the real subject of *Christabel*. Although Coleridge projects himself primarily into the character of Christabel, every character in the poem is endowed with and suffers from an intensely ambivalent nature. Thus, although unfinished, the poem yet reveals a unifying design, a design dictated by Coleridge's fixation on and identification with the ambivalent mother.

A Reading

Although the composition and publication of *Christabel* extended over a four-year period, between 1797 and 1801, and although never completed, the poem can nevertheless be considered unified. Coleridge himself stresses that his conception of the poem had always been whole in his mind: "The reason of my not finishing *Christabel* is not that I don't know how to do it — for I have, as I always had, the whole plan entire from beginning to end in my mind; but I fear I cannot carry on with equal success the execution of the idea, an extremely subtle and difficult one."[10] This "idea," as we shall see, concerns an unconscious conflict that indeed involves subtle and difficult emotions. The danger to the ego of uncovering these threatening emotions perhaps accounts for Coleridge's inability to proceed further with the poem than he did. Regardless of his reasons for not completing it, since he did see the two Parts and the Conclusion as belonging to a single idea, I feel justified in beginning my analysis with the Conclusion. The feelings expressed in this brief last section expose, in a clear and direct manner, the feelings animating the more obscurely complicated drama of the two preceding sections.

The Conclusion opens with the portrait of a child, a vision the poet considers blissfully ideal:

> A little child, a limber elf,
> Singing, dancing to itself,
> A fairy thing with red round cheeks,
> That always finds, and never seeks,
> Makes such a vision to the sight
> As fills a father's eyes with light;

Coleridge significantly highlights the child's complete autonomy and self-sufficiency. It is singing and dancing "to itself," and it "never seeks." In an earlier version, Coleridge emphasizes this feature by italicizing the words *finds* and *seeks*. Apparently, the child is also amply nourished, for it has "red round cheeks." These characteristics of the child curiously oppose those of Christabel in Parts One and Two. Christabel always seeks and never finds; she is always seeking a love that is absent—her absent knight, her absent mother, and, in Part Two, the love of her angry father. Also unlike the child, Christabel is pale and wan, and, by the end, wasted and shrinking. The vision of the child is a vision of an ideally fulfilled self, a condition that the poem as a whole recognizes as impossible. For it is the unfulfilled love and the intense

pain and rage it incites that is the real subject of *Christabel* and the
subject of the remainder of the Conclusion. Coleridge describes
the child's father, whose heart overflows with love for the child,
and yet he

> . . . at last
> Must needs express his love's excess
> With words of unmeant bitterness.
> . . . .
> Perhaps 'tis tender too and pretty
> At each wild word to feel within
> A sweet recoil of love and pity.
> And what, if in a world of sin
> (O sorrow and shame should this be true!)
> Such giddiness of heart and brain
> Comes seldom save from rage and pain,
> . . . .

Coleridge here and throughout the poem is deeply troubled by
what he recognizes as a mysterious, intimate connection between
"love's excess" and a bitter, aggressive rage. It is significantly an
excessive love that results in the wild and bitter words. The love is
most likely felt to be excessive because it is more than can be
accepted or reciprocated by the love object; it is a needy and de-
manding love that causes shame. Coleridge intuitively recognizes
that at the source of this "giddiness of heart and brain," this mael-
strom of love and hate, is the "rage and pain" of unfulfilled love.

The three main characters in *Christabel* — Geraldine, Christabel, and Sir Leoline — all embody the intensely ambivalent condition described in the Conclusion. In Part Two, "pain and rage" is
indeed the most oft-repeated phrase. The fact that Christabel is
female, furthermore, may be due not only to an attempted disguise,
as Wormhoudt suggests, but also to a closer identification with the
loved and hated mother whose presence dominates the poem. As
Kernberg and others have shown, a fixation on and identification
with the mother imago is a typical response to an early frustration
and ambivalence in the mother-child relationship. This internal
psychic conflict also bears on the overall form and style of the
poem. The ballad form, with its repetitions and simple rocking
rhythms, is a good vehicle, as Beverly Fields has pointed out, for
unconscious primitive feelings.[11] Being an ancient and traditional

form, it also allows the poet to feel safely distanced from the emotionally threatening material. The supernatural mode further enables Coleridge to avoid dealing directly with Nature/mother in his poetry. Yet as Harding observes in his analysis of *The Ancient Mariner*, the supernatural machinery often does have a real correspondence with inner psychological workings. The mariner's small, impulsive act, for instance, "which presses the supernatural trigger," Harding asserts, "does form an effective parallel to the hidden impulse which has such a devastating meaning for one's irrational, and partly unconscious, private standards."[12] In *Christabel* the supernatural transformations are comparable to the irrational displacements and condensations that occur in dreams. A Gothic tale of terror is ultimately the form most suitable for Coleridge's deepest nightmare.

The first part of *Christabel*, as Knight has noted, is indeed "strangely feminine." The images with which Coleridge introduces the tale have associations that are at once feminine, passive, deathly, and sinister. It is the middle of the night. Whereas the male cock is crowing only "drowsily," the baron's "toothless mastiff bitch" is howling as if "she sees my lady's shroud" (6-13). It is apparent from later revisions that Coleridge troubled over the destructive aggression exposed in these lines, specifically over the offensive connotations of the word *bitch*. He changed the lines "Sir Leoline, the Baron rich, / Hath a toothless mastiff bitch" first to "Sir Leoline, the Baron bold / Hath a toothless mastiff old," and then finally to "Sir Leoline, the Baron rich, / Hath a toothless mastiff which." Wormhoudt believes that *which* can be read as *witch*. If so read, the lines express the same unconscious rage as they do in the original version.

The stanza that immediately follows presents another feminine image in hostile and aggressive shades. Coleridge describes the night as "chilly" but not as completely dark, for "The thin gray cloud is spread on high, / It covers but not hides the sky, / The moon is behind, and at the full; / And yet she looks both small and dull." As in Keats's poetry, the moon is a prominent and heavily loaded image in Coleridge's work; it figures always as an ever-watchful maternal presence. In *The Ancient Mariner*, for instance, the rising of an ominous "horned Moon" heralds the entrance of the Nightmare Life-in-Death. Yet it is by the light of a graciously shining moon that the mariner beholds the water snakes and consequently redeems himself by blessing them, and when the "thick black cloud" subsequently pours down a reparative rain, "The Moon was at its side." (Other aspects of Coleridge's moon image will be discussed later in an analysis of *Frost at Midnight*.) In *Christabel*, the moon resides in a chilly night and is significantly "small and dull." The moon/mother, in other words, is denying her light/milk; she is cold, withdrawn, and shrunken. This withdrawn and shrunken image forms a recurring motif in the poem — from Geraldine's lean and shrunken bosom to Christabel's "dull" and "shrunken serpent eyes" at the end.

Thus, the angry and destructive feelings toward the mother which are imagistically revealed in the setting preface Christabel's entrance into the woods and affect the action that takes place there. Christabel is going to the woods to pray because "She had dreams all yesternight / Of her own betrothed knight; / And she in the midnight wood will pray / For the weal of her lover that's far away" (27-30). In the first edition of the poem, the agitating and erotic nature of these dreams is emphasized: "Dreams that made her moan and leap, / As on her bed she lay in sleep." Christabel feels that she must pray for the welfare of her absent lover apparently because her dreams have led her to fear him harm. In other words, she is perhaps afraid of the damaging powers revealed in her own disturbingly erotic/destructive dreams. The absent knight, furthermore, is intimately connected with Geraldine, for it is Geraldine who appears to Christabel as a result of her night journey to pray; Geraldine appears indeed as if in answer to the prayer. As we shall see shortly, she is also inextricably connected with Christabel's dead mother. Christabel's prayer, then, like the poet's supplication in *Pains of Sleep*, is really addressed to the loved and hated mother. Her praying under a "broad-breasted" oak tree enforces this idea.

Christabel's first vision of Geraldine, as she spies her lying behind the oak, is at once beautiful and terrifying. Coleridge invokes "Jesu, Maria" to "shield her well!"

> There she sees a damsel bright,
> Drest in a silken robe of white,
> That shadowy in the moonlight shone:
> The neck that made that white robe wan,
> Her stately neck, and arms were bare;

Her blue-veined feet unsandal'd were,
And wildly glittered here and there
The gems entangled in her hair.

[58-65]

The aspect of Geraldine's appearance which Coleridge first emphasizes—her "silken robe of white" which shines in the moonlight
—associates the "damsel bright" with the white light of the moon
itself. Coleridge refers more than once to Geraldine's "vestments
white," and throughout the poem she is generally associated with
whiteness. She tells Christabel, for instance, of the white steeds of
the warriors and of how they tied her to a "palfrey white." Her
whiteness suggests not only moon/mother but also breast/milk.
The initial portrait of Geraldine hints at qualities that are both
erotic and incipiently violent and destructive. Coleridge describes
the lady's bare neck and arms and particularly highlights her bare
"blue-veined feet." Considering the poet's recurrent nightmare
image of being trampled, emphasis on the bared feet is significant;
certainly the feet have destructive, perhaps phallic, associations.
Finally, the "wildly" glittering gems that are "entangled" in her
hair also suggest erotic as well as unbridled and potentially violent
passions. Christabel exclaims that "twas frightful" to see a lady so
beautiful and richly clad, and she cries, "Mary mother, save me
now!" As Geraldine embodies both the desired and ideal good
mother and the feared and vengeful bad mother, so the mother-
image is split generally between the good and the bad throughout
the poem. Christabel frequently appeals to the image of the
idealized good mother to defend her from the bad. She is
threatened, not only by the bad mother in Geraldine, but by the
bad mother within herself, due to her internalization of and identification with that object of her obsessive desire and terror.

Geraldine indeed allows Christabel the opportunity to act out
the mother role herself. The mother-child parts alternate between
them throughout the poem. At the beginning, Christabel finds
Geraldine in a weak and helpless state, having been seized and
abandoned by the wicked warriors. Geraldine's position is thus
initially that of a forlorn and abandoned child. Coleridge describes
how Christabel "stretched forth her hand, / And comforted fair
Geraldine" and promised to "guide and guard" her "safe and free"
(104-10). Christabel thus acts the comforting and protecting

mother. Coleridge extends this image even further as he describes Christabel and Geraldine crossing the moat:

> They crossed the moat, and Christabel
> Took the key that fitted well;
> A little door she opened straight,
> All in the middle of the gate;
> The gate that was ironed within and without,
> Where an army in battle array had marched out.
> The lady sank, belike through pain,
> And Christabel, with might and main
> Lifted her up, a weary weight,
> Over the threshold of the gate:
> Then the lady rose again,
> And moved, as she were not in pain.
>
> [123-34]

As Beres has pointed out, the passage reveals some unmistakable birth imagery. With a mighty effort, Christabel carries Geraldine over the threshold, delivering her through the portal. Once in the court, Coleridge states, then repeats, that they were now "free from danger, free from fear" (135, 143). The statement is, of course, ironical. It serves perhaps as a defensive denial of the very fear and danger that is always present for Coleridge in the mother-child relationship.

The fearful and dangerous aspect of that relationship is immediately betrayed when Christabel proposes that they "move as if in stealth" (120) so as not to wake the ailing Sir Leoline. In an earlier version the lines read, "So to my room we'll creep in stealth." Certainly the fear of the father has oedipal undertones. Nevertheless, the essential emotional conflict is still preoedipal. Christabel's guilty stealth is due less to a guilty oedipal desire than to a more primitive, greedy desire for the mother's exclusive attention. In Part Two, Christabel's attitude toward her father suggests that she merely redirects this same desire toward him. Sir Leoline himself will be seen to be less a retaliatory oedipal father than, once again, a loved and hated mother-figure. Christabel's feelings of shame and guilt, then, arise from the angry and aggressive nature of her greedy love.

After Christabel and Geraldine cross the court, Christabel's, or Coleridge's, anxiety begins to surface more forcefully. The mastiff bitch, first of all, asleep in the "moonshine cold," awakes and makes an "angry moan." Then as Geraldine passes the hall where the brands lay dying "Amid their own white ashes,"

> . . . there came
> A tongue of light, a fit of flame;
> And Christabel saw the lady's eye,
> And nothing else saw she thereby,
> Save the boss of the shield of Sir Leoline tall,
> Which hung in a murky niche in the wall.
>
> [159-63]

Ocular imagery is prominent throughout the poem, and the connection here among the "lady's eye," the "white ashes," and the "tongue of light" suggests a psychological explanation. In this passage, oral images immediately precede the illumination of Geraldine's eye; white, as discussed, associates in Coleridge's mind with breast/milk, and the "tongue of light" further enforces the oral idea. Voyeurism is rooted in the oral disposition; the desire to get and "drink in" with the eyes is akin to the oral wish. As Wormhoudt explains, "The voyeur uses his eyes to take in forbidden sights just as the lips are used to suck at the breast." Kohut has also written about the oral-visual relationship. If the mother physically and emotionally recoils from the child, if she withholds her body, he says, the visual will become hypercathectic for the child.[13] The oral-eye images in the above passage also project a distinctly ominous light. The dying brands and ashes, the flamed tongue, and the portentous "evil" eye reflect the enraged and ambivalent feelings at the root of the oral experience. That Christabel's only other sight is of the boss of Sir Leoline's shield, which Wormhoudt sees as another breast image, emphasizes the fear of retaliation which accompanies the greedy and destructive oral wish. In the final lines of the stanza, Christabel anxiously reminds Geraldine to "softly tread" for her father "seldom sleepeth well."

Once they reach Christabel's chamber, however, the fear and anxieties only become more urgent, for the threat comes less from the father than from the ambivalent mother. As they enter the room, Coleridge again mentions the "dim" moon. Although its beams cannot enter the room, the chamber is nevertheless provided with its own moon—a "silver lamp" that "burns dead and dim"

(186). Thus, the cold and deathly moon/mother image again appears. The lamp exhibits another forboding feature: a silver chain "fastened to an angel's feet." If we recall the phallic and destructive associations that feet have for Coleridge, the ambivalent nature of the moon image here becomes all the more apparent. It is in the light of this ambivalent mother image that the climactic scene between Geraldine and Christabel unfolds.

Christabel offers Geraldine a drink: "I pray you, drink this cordial wine! / It is a wine of virtuous powers; / My mother made it of wild flowers" (191-93). The drink causes Geraldine's "fair large eyes" to "glitter bright." Although the scene reverses the oral experience, with Christabel again assuming the mother's role, the manifest emotions are still the child's (Christabel's and Coleridge's) fears of and ambivalence toward the mother. The wine, first of all, was made by Christabel's mother. When Geraldine is informed of this, she asks, "And will your mother pity me, / Who am a maiden most forlorn?" The mother, however, is incapable of love and pity for the forlorn child. As Christabel explains, "She died the hour that I was born." The child indeed feels guiltily responsible for the mother's death. In the mother's deathbed prophecy, which Christabel describes to Geraldine, the fear of punishment is evident: "I have heard the grey-haired friar tell / How on her death-bed she did say, / That she would hear the castle-bell / Strike twelve upon my wedding-day" (198-202).

The tolling of the castle bell is associated throughout the poem with death: the mastiff bitch howls in answer to the clock "as if she sees my lady's shroud," and in Part Two, the Baron declares, "Each matin bell . . . Knells us back to a world of death" (332-33). Christabel fears retaliation for her unconscious destruction of her mother. That fear is projected onto Geraldine who now assumes the form of the vengeful, bad mother. In her fear of the bad mother, Christabel again appeals to the image of the good mother—"O mother dear! that thou wert here!"—but Geraldine as the bad mother image prevails. She commands, "'Off, wandering mother! Peak and pine! / I have power to bid thee flee,'" and "with hollow voice," she cries, "Off, woman, off! this hour is mine— / Though thou her guardian spirit be, / Off, woman, off! 'tis given to me.'" (204-13). Geraldine then orders Christabel to unrobe herself and lie beside her. The two recline, but Christabel is restless and succumbs to a desire to rise up and "look at the lady Geraldine."

The desire to look, as discussed, is akin to the oral wish to take in. Christabel is thus to be punished for her greedy desire to "look" at Geraldine. The scene that follows vividly expresses the anger and terror associated with the original oral experience:

> Beneath the lamp the lady bowed,
> And slowly rolled her eyes around;
> Then drawing in her breath aloud,
> Like one that shuddered, she unbound
> The cincture from beneath her breast:
> Her silken robe, and inner vest,
> Dropt to her feet, and full in view,
> Behold! her bosom and half her side—
> A sight to dream of, not to tell!
> O shield her, shield sweet Christabel!
>
> [245-54]

In an earlier version, Coleridge describes the breasts even more explicitly as "lean and old and foul of hue." It is reportedly at this point that Shelley, while attending a reading of the poem, hallucinated eyes in Mary Godwin's nipples and fled the room in terror.[14] The incident is revealing both of Shelley's personality and of the psychological structure of the poem. Clearly it exemplifies the general oral-voyeuristic association. Shelley obviously identified with Christabel and his confused terror simply mirrors that of Christabel herself. Finally, Geraldine proclaims, "In the touch of this bosom there worketh a spell / Which is lord of thy utterance, Christabel!" The bad, denying mother thus takes her revenge.

The Conclusion to Part One serves only to reinforce the presiding power of the good-bad mother image. Coleridge returns to the image of Christabel "Kneeling in the moonlight" at the old oak tree:

> It was a lovely sight to see
> The lady Christabel, when she
> Was praying at the old oak tree.
>   Amid the jagged shadows
>   Of mossy leafless boughs,
>   Kneeling in the moonlight,
>   To make her gentle vows;
> . . . .
>
> [279-85]

The sight is no longer so "lovely," however, for the shadows are pointedly "jagged" and the boughs "leafless." Neither is the image of Christabel herself so innocent and pleasing as before. She is "Asleep, and dreaming fearfully," as she is at the beginning of the poem, but now she is dreaming "with open eyes (ah woe is me!) . . . Dreaming that alone, which is— / O sorrow and shame! Can this be she, / The lady, who knelt at the old oak tree?" (292-97). Christabel is now confronting with open eyes those destructive and shameful dreams concerning the mother. She only "seems to slumber still and mild" in Geraldine's arms. Moreover, Coleridge explicitly likens the scene to that of "a mother with her child" (300).

The final stanza of the Conclusion to Part One makes one last appeal to the good mother image. Although Christabel's sleep is unquiet and full of fearful dreams, she is yet, Coleridge says, "praying always"—she "prays in sleep" (322). The restlessness, he continues, "'tis but the blood so free / Comes back and tingles in her feet." The remark, with its allusion to the maiden's feet, only further betrays the unconscious destructive passions that are the real disturbance to sleep. The poet, however, concludes,

> What if her guardian spirit 'twere,
> What if she knew her mother near?
> But this she knows, in joys and woes,
> That saints will aid if men will call:
> For the blue sky bends over all!

Coleridge thus ends hopefully, with the benevolent maternal image of a blue sky bending attentively and lovingly over all.

Part One was completed in 1797. Three years later Coleridge published Part Two. The unconscious emotional conflicts that shaped Part One nevertheless remained active through the years, and Part Two picks up the threads of the earlier section. The second part, however, does indicate some psychological progress. Whereas Part One concentrates primarily on the terrifying and ambivalent figure of Geraldine, the focus of Part Two is increasingly inward, on the ambivalence, the guilt and shame within Christabel herself. The poem displays Coleridge's developing awareness of the destructive feelings within himself and his growing ability to take responsibility for them.

Part Two opens with a reminder of the mother's death and thus of Christabel's murderous and guilty feelings:

> Each matin bell, the Baron saith,
> Knells us back to a world of death.
> These words Sir Leoline first said,
> When he rose and found his lady dead:
> These words Sir Leoline will say
> Many a morn to his dying day!

Christabel thus associates the father with the mother's revenge. She indeed comes to identify the father with the same loving/ vengeful mother. Yet the mother/father figure is less guilty of vengeful feelings than is Christabel herself. Describing Christabel waking beside Geraldine in the morning, Coleridge writes, "And Christabel awoke and spied / The same who lay down by her side— / O rather say, the same whom she / Raised up beneath the old oak tree!" (369-72). Why "rather say" that Christabel "raised up" Geraldine than that Geraldine "lay down by her side"? The altered phrasing, which makes Christabel the active subject, clearly places the responsibility for the previous night's terror with her. She cries, "Sure I have sinn'd!'" and she greets Geraldine "with such perplexity of mind / As dreams too lively leave behind" (381-86). Christabel is troubled and bewildered by her own unconscious violent emotions.

The baron's role in the drama further excites Christabel's confusion and anxiety, and his character again gives expression to the poem's central ambivalent conflict. Sir Leoline discovers that Geraldine is the daughter of Lord Roland, the estranged friend of his youth. Where once Roland had been "his heart's best brother," the two had quarreled and parted, "ne'er to meet again." Coleridge comments, "And to be wroth with one we love / Doth work like madness in the brain." The madness is indeed Christabel's own. The baron only incites that madness by again acting the role of the rejecting parent. Leoline's anger and hatred toward Roland turns easily back to love (the hate being only a product of frustrated love in the first place), and he embraces Geraldine as a long lost child. It is precisely this embrace, however, that Christabel herself covets, and thus the sight of it fills her with a furious envy. Although her jealousy could be interpreted oedipally (Christabel as the disguised Coleridge witnessing the father's embrace of the mother), Leoline's relation to Geraldine as to a child, referring to her always as "the child of his friend," suggests that Christabel's jealousy has a more infantile source.

Christabel's fury toward the denying mother/father figure, however, only turns back on her; she feels guilty for her enraged hostility and fears retaliation. Leoline swears revenge on the warriors who seized Geraldine and vows that he will "dislodge their reptile souls," and as he speaks, Coleridge says, "his eye in lightening rolls!" (442-44). Because of the oral-voyeuristic connection, the child's fear is again expressed in the parent's evil, vengeful eye. Christabel is further threatened by the father's promised revenge in that the reference to the "reptile souls" associates not only with Geraldine, but, as we shall see, with Christabel herself. When Christabel views Leoline and Geraldine's embrace, Coleridge describes:

> Again she saw that bosom old,
> Again she felt that bosom cold,
> And drew in her breath with a hissing sound:
> Whereat the Knight turned wildly round,
> And nothing saw, but his own sweet maid
> With eyes upraised, as one that prayed.
>
> [456-62]

The sight of the embrace stirs up the same enraged envy that the child originally experienced in relation to the mother who withheld all her love, warmth, and milk. In this passage, however, it is not Geraldine who reveals the cold reptilian aspect but Christabel herself, who "drew in her breath with a hissing sound." Christabel, like the mother image, is split between the ideal and the malevolent, divided by her ambivalent feelings. As Coleridge makes increasingly clear, the serpentine, bad mother resides in the heart of the seemingly innocent "sweet maid."

Reptilian imagery is ubiquitous throughout Part Two. The image of the snake, as Sloane observes, has traditionally been associated with ambivalent earth-goddesses. Besides its obvious phallic associations, the snake's curved and sinuous aspect relates it to a woman's body. It is thus a perfect image for the phallic, or ambivalent, woman. Leoline's bard Barcy, who has been instructed to report to Lord Roland that his daughter is "safe and free" (echoing Christabel's ironic words), hesitates because of a strange dream he has had concerning a snake and a dove. He wishes to delay his journey,

> For in my sleep I saw that dove,
> That gentle bird, whom thou dost love,
> And call'st by thy own daughter's name—
> Sir Leoline! I saw the same
> Fluttering, and uttering fearful moan,
> Among the green herbs in the forest alone.
> . . . .
> I stooped, methought, the dove to take,
> When lo! I saw a bright green snake
> Coiled around its wings and neck.
> Green as the herbs on which it couched,
> Close by the dove's head it crouched;
> And with the dove it heaves and stirs,
> Swelling its neck as she swelled hers!
> I woke; it was the midnight hour,
> The clock was echoing in the tower;
> . . . .

[531-36, 548-56]

The clock again tolls as a reminder of the mother's death and thus of Christabel's guilty, destructive feelings. In this passage, Christabel is imaged as the innocent dove who is being destroyed by the phallic mother. In the stanza that follows, however, Leoline addresses Geraldine as "Lord Roland's beauteous dove" and promises to "crush the snake" (569-71). The threat terrifies Christabel and triggers the following fantasy. Coleridge describes how Geraldine "couched her head upon her breast, / And looked askance at Christabel." He again invokes "Jesu, Maria" to "shield" Christabel from the terrible mother:

> A snake's small eye blinks dull and shy;
> And the lady's eyes they shrunk in her head,
> Each shrunk up to a serpent's eye,
> And with somewhat of malice, and more of dread,
> At Christabel she looked askance!—
> One moment—and the sight was fled!

[583-88]

The description combines the "dull" and "shrunken" moon image with that of the serpent, and again the terror is associated with the eyes. The bad mother's glance, however, contains only "somewhat of malice" but "more of dread." She is less terrible than terrified herself. It is Christabel's, or the child's, own violent and destructive feelings that are the real source of dread; she fears most the serpent within herself. Christabel "shuddered aloud, with a hissing sound," and Coleridge describes,

> The maid, alas! her thoughts are gone,
> She nothing sees—no sight but one!
> The maid, devoid of guile and sin,
> I know not how, in fearful wise,
> So deeply has she drunken in
> That look, those shrunken serpent eyes,
> That all her features were resigned
> To this sole image in her mind:
> And passively did imitate
> That look of dull and treacherous hate!
> And thus she stood, in dizzy trance,
> Still picturing that look askance
> With forced unconscious sympathy
> Full before her father's view—
> As far as such a look could be
> In eyes so innocent and blue!
>
> [597-612]

The passage reveals a profound psychological insight. Coleridge intuitively recognizes the internalization and identification with the bad mother imago, the "forced unconscious sympathy," that results from the child's frustrated oral need to take in and possess. Christabel had "so deeply . . . drunken in . . . those shrunken serpent eyes" that she becomes possessed by the hateful, treacherous image—it indeed becomes the "sole image in her mind." The child is thus not simply victim, but is herself deeply culpable.

Finally, Christabel implores the Baron, "'By my mother's soul do I entreat / That thou this woman send away.'" For the sake of the good mother, in other words, he must rid her of the bad. Sir Leoline, however, suffers from the same paralyzing ambivalence as Christabel. "His heart was cleft with pain and rage," his bosom swelled with "confusion," "his eyes were wild," and his cheek "wan and wild" (621-41). The poet himself pleads with the baron:

> Why is thy cheek so wan and wild,
> Sir Leoline? Thy only child
> Lies at thy feet, thy joy, thy pride,
> So fair, so innocent, so mild;
> The same, for whom thy lady died!
> O by the pangs of her dear mother
> Think thou no evil of thy child!
>
> [621-25]

By emphasizing Christabel's alliance with the dead mother here, Coleridge only stresses again the child's ambivalence and guilt. The rest of the stanza further accents this alliance as Coleridge discusses how the mother "Prayed that the babe for whom she died, / Might prove her dear lord's joy and pride!" Coleridge concludes, "And woulds't thou wrong thy only child, / Her child and thine?" (635). By stressing once more the child's association with the mother—it is "Her child" as well as his—Coleridge again identifies the ambivalent mother with Christabel, who is thus forced to suffer the consequences. The baron feels disgraced and "Dishonoured by his only child." He rolls "his eye with stern regard," orders the bard on his mission, and ultimately rejects and abandons Christabel as he leads the lady Geraldine from the room. Thus Christabel is punished by being made to suffer the same rejection and abandonment, the same traumatizing treatment, that originally excited her ambivalence and guilt. It is ultimately the retribution she expects.

After Christabel receives her due punishment, Coleridge perhaps no longer felt compelled to continue with the poem. Yet even in his proposed ending, which James Gilman reports,[15] the central theme of ambivalent love continues. Coleridge considered ending the poem by having Geraldine leave the court to return disguised as Christabel's lover. Christabel was to be strangely repelled by "his" advances, and the action was finally to be resolved by the appearance of the true lover, at which point Geraldine as the false lover would disappear. The proposed ending thus supports the interpretation of Geraldine as Christabel's ambivalent love object. The beloved is both good and bad, true and false, desired and feared. Coleridge apparently had planned to exorcise the bad mother image. The task evidently proved more difficult than he anticipated.

The problem of ambivalent love is also the subject of several other lyrics written during the same period as *Christabel*. While at work on *Christabel*, Coleridge was also preparing *Love* (first published as *Introduction to the Tale of the Dark Ladie*) and *The Ballad of the Dark Ladie*. In *Love*, a knight woos his lady Genevieve by telling her the tale of a "bold and lovely knight" who was "crazed" by the "cruel scorn" of his dark lady. The lovesick knight finally wins his dark lady by a heroic but "murderous" act:

> There came and looked him in the face
> An angel beautiful and bright;
> And that he knew it was a Fiend,
>   This miserable Knight!
>
> And that unknowing what he did,
> He leaped amid a murderous band,
> And saved from outrage worse than death
>   The Lady of the Land!
>
> [49-56]

As in so many of Byron's tales, the Romantic hero, due to his ambivalent love, is led into a destructive act. Whereas Byron's stories usually end with the hero overcome by guilt and despair, Coleridge's *Love* expresses a wishful fantasy. The dark lady is so repentant and grateful for her rescue, she "ever strove to expiate / The scorn that crazed his brain" and "nursed him in a cave." Genevieve is so "disturbed . . . with pity" by this tale, and particularly by the thought of the knight's "dying words," that she rushes into the arms of her own knight, and the poem concludes, "And so I won my Genevieve, / My bright and beauteous Bride." The fantasy again exposes Coleridge's craving for a mother who would nurse, comfort, and pity him.

In *The Ballad of the Dark Ladie* it is the dark lady herself who both needs and fears the maternal love. She sends her page "Up the castled mountain's breast" to find her betrothed knight. Once reunited, she begs her beloved to "give me shelter in thy breast! / O shield and shelter me!" The knight proposes that they "steal" through the dark together. The proposal, however, terrifies the lady and she cries:

The dark? the dark? No! not the dark?
The twinkling stars? How, Henry? How?
O God! 'twas in the eye of noon
    He pledged his sacred vow!

And in the eye of noon my love
Shall lead me from my mother's door,
. . . .

[45-50]

Like Christabel, the dark lady is at once identified with and yet terrified of the bad, "dark" mother.

Finally, *Lewti, or the Circassian Love-Chaunt*, published in 1798, also centers on the image of an all-powerful and ambivalent woman. The poet is "dying" for love of the fair but "treacherous" Lewti. The poem plays variations on the refrain, "Image of Lewti! from my mind / Depart, for Lewti is not kind." The woman is again associated with the moon, and the poet here identifies himself with a pale, thin cloud that is floating toward it:

I saw a cloud of palest hue,
    Onward to the moon it passed;
Still brighter and more bright it grew,
With floating colours not a few,
    Till it reached the moon at last:
Then the cloud was wholly bright,
With a rich and amber light!
And so with many a hope I seek,
    And with such joy I find my Lewti
And even so my pale wan cheek
    Drinks in as deep a flush of beauty!
Nay, treacherous image! leave my mind,
If Lewti never will be kind

[25-37]

Like the cloud that is not "wholly bright" until it reaches the moon, the poet, in his deepest self, feels whole and alive only when reflected in the light of the mother's eyes or when he can "drink in" her love. In the manuscript version of the poem, the poet avows that "pity dwells in Lewti's breast" if only he "knew how to find it," if only he could "see my Lewti's eyes" shining through the thin mist of the cloud. This same yearning to see the mother's eyes and to feel the self sympathetically illuminated by them is most poignantly expressed in *Frost at Midnight*. Although that poem, one of Coleridge's most successful, exposes the narcissistic wound and expresses deep feelings of pain and loss, it is not impaired by uncontrolled infantile anger, self-pity, or the desire for regressive fusion. In *Frost at Midnight* Coleridge allows the mother her separateness while yet longing for an empathetic response. The poem envisions an active, mirroring relationship in which both the mother and the self remain intact.

FROST AT MIDNIGHT:
THE MIRRORING RELATIONSHIP
OF SELF AND MOTHER

Just as Christabel is always seeking or praying for an absent love, so the sense of absence, of deep but unfocused loss, pervades *Frost at Midnight*. The first stanza creates the impression of a rich and mysterious life that is happening all around the poet but is yet inaccessible to him.

> The Frost performs its secret ministry,
> Unhelped by any wind. The owlet's cry
> Came loud—and hark, again! loud as before
> The inmates of my cottage, all at rest,
> Have left me to that solitude, which suits
> Abstruser musings: . . .

The poet feels abandoned, isolated, out of touch. The inmates of his cottage are "all at rest" and have "left" him to this restless solitude. The same feeling also permeates *This Lime-Tree Bower My Prison*, which begins, "Well, they are gone, and here must I remain, / This lime-tree bower my prison! I have lost / Beauties and feelings, such as would have been / Most sweet to my remembrance . . ." In *Frost at Midnight* the poet sits alone beside his cradled infant while outside "The Frost performs its secret ministry." Nature, in other words, is cold, remote, and unknowable, performing her ministrations in a world outside the poet's grasp. The solitary stillness indeed "disturbs" and "vexes" the poet:

> 'Tis calm indeed! so calm, that it disturbs
> And vexes meditation with its strange

And extreme silentness. Sea, hill, and wood,
This populous village! Sea, hill, and wood,
With all the numberless goings-on of life,
Inaudible as dreams!

[8-13]

The calm, the "extreme silentness," is frustrating because it
indicates an unresponsive and indifferent environment. Nature's
abundance and vitality, its "numberless goings-on," the "populous"
life of "Sea, hill, and wood" are as remote and "inaudible" to the
speaker as he must feel the demands or cries of his own life are
inaudible to it. Behind the pervading feeling of abandonment and
loss in Coleridge's poetry is always the primal subjective experience of maternal deprivation and exclusion. Even those features of
Nature which Coleridge chooses to specify—"Sea, hill, and wood"
—are pointedly feminine and maternal. It is also worth noting that
in *This Lime-Tree Bower* the injury responsible for the poet's
confinement was inflicted by his wife; prior to the outing, Sara
Coleridge had spilled scalding milk on her husband's foot. Considering the loaded symbolic value that both feet and milk have
for Coleridge, the incident could not but have aroused deep feelings
of unresolved rage over the original narcissistic injury. Although
no such actual incident prefaces *Frost at Midnight*, the narcissistic
wound nevertheless propels the composition of that poem as well.
By the end of *Frost at Midnight*, however, the poet manages to
transcend his enraged feelings of loss. In the process of identifying
with his infant and imagining a more generous and expansive
existence for this second infant self, Coleridge, at least momentarily, finds relief from the angry, ruptured relations that fet-
ter his own internal life.

The first half of the poem expresses the familiar Romantic
yearning for an ideal, or second, self. The poet musingly identifies
with the fluttering film on the grate of the fire, "the sole unquiet
thing . . . in this hush of nature." The act of identification moves
the poet to reflect on "the idling Spirit" that "By its own moods
interprets every where / Echo or mirror seeking of itself." (20-22).
As is evident from the manuscript version, Coleridge labored long
over this idea. In the earlier version, he speaks of the "living spirit
in our frame" which "Transfuses into all its own delight, / Its own
volition," often "with most superstitious wish." The wish for a

magical identification with the object and the longing for an "echo" or "mirror" of the self characterize the infant's fantasies of narcissistic omnipotence and its narcissistic idealizations. Throughout his poetry, Coleridge displays a troubled concern with his propensity for idealized narcissistic projections. In *Constancy to an Ideal Object* (1826?), for instance, he addresses the ideal Thought of his beloved and differentiates it from the actual woman herself—"Yet still thou haunt'st me; and though well I see, / She is not thou, and only thou art she." He concludes,

> And art thou nothing? Such thou art, as when
> The woodman winding westward up the glen
> At wintry dawn, where o'er the sheep-track's maze
> The viewless snow-mist weaves a glist'ning haze,
> Sees full before him gliding without tread,
> An image with a glory round its head;
> The enamoured rustic worships its fair hues,
> Nor knows he makes the shadow, he pursues!

In *Phantom or Fact* (1830?), Coleridge reveals the intimate connection between the images of the ideal love object, the ideal self, and the ambivalent mother. The poet imagines that a "lovely form" sat beside his bed, shedding a "feeding calm." The form, he explains, "'Twas my own spirit newly come from heaven." The shape is thus associated with both a "feeding" maternal presence and an ideal self. In this case, however, the idealization is shattered by the underlying ambivalence:

> Alas! that change how fain would I forget!
> That shrinking back, like one that had mistook!
> That weary, wandering, disavowing look!
> 'Twas all another, feature, look, and frame,
> And still, methought, I knew, it was the same!

As in *Christabel*, Coleridge dramatizes the schizoid condition—the split between a good and a bad self which results from the internalization of the ambivalent mother imago.

The longing for a twin, or second, self which *Frost at Midnight* expresses stems from this same internal split. The second self may be understood as the projected good or loved self, the true self never acknowledged by the mother. This becomes even more apparent in the third stanza as Coleridge pursues the associations of

the fluttering film. Such films, commonly called "strangers," were
supposed to portend the arrival of some absent friend. Coleridge
describes how often at school, while watching the stranger, he
would drift into dreams of his "sweet birth-place," of "soothing
things" that "lulled" him into a deep sleep. The stranger is thus
associated with a regressive return to an ideal mother and also, as
the final lines of the stanza make clear, with the twin self-image.
For "if the door half opened," Coleridge says, ". . . still my heart
leaped up, / For still I hoped to see the stanger's face, / Townsman,
or aunt, or sister more beloved, / My play-mate when we both
were clothed alike!" (40-45).

With the fourth stanza, the poet turns to his cradled babe and
addresses his thoughts directly to it:

> My babe so beautiful! it thrills my heart
> With tender gladness, thus to look at thee,
> And think that thou shalt learn far other lore,
> And in far other scenes! For I was reared
> In the great city, pent 'mid cloisters dim,
> And saw nought lovely but the sky and stars.
>
> [48-53]

As in *This Lime-Tree Bower*, the poet feels imprisoned and cut off
from Nature. Although he provides a literal reason for this alienation, having been "reared in the great city," the fact, much as the
injury in *This Lime-Tree Bower*, does not preclude a still deeper
emotional source. The rift in Coleridge's relation with Nature is
not due simply to his having been raised in the city, but to the
deeper lack of empathy which he experienced in relation to his
first maternal environment. The poet thus hopes that his child will
have that communion with Nature which was denied him:

> But *thou*, my babe! shalt wander like a breeze
> By lakes and sandy shores, beneath the crags
> Of ancient mountain, and beneath the clouds,
> Which image in their bulk both lakes and shores
> And mountain crags: . . .
>
> [54-58]

The image of the clouds that mirror the shapes of the earth
below suggests a sympathetic "reflecting" Nature. Like the clouds,
his babe, Coleridge asserts, shall also reflect and be enlightened by

Nature's, or God's, eternal love: "so shalt thou see and hear / The lovely shapes and sounds intelligible / Of that eternal language, . . ." The thought is similar to that in *The Eolian Harp* when Coleridge speaks of "the one Life within us and abroad / Which meets all motion and becomes its soul." In that poem, however, Coleridge reveals that such a meeting or union with the Eternal Power cannot occur within him, "For never guiltless may I speak of him, / The Incomprehensible." He himself, he claims, is "A sinful and most miserable man, / Wilder'd and dark" (56-62). Thus, in *Frost at Midnight*, by projecting himself into his innocent child, Coleridge is able to imaginatively reestablish a relationship with Nature that is not overshadowed by his feelings of hostility and guilt. Even here, though, as we will see from the manuscript version of the poem, Coleridge had to work through his anger and aggression. The last stanza of the final version, however, testifies to the successful resolution of those feelings:

> Therefore all seasons shall be sweet to thee,
> Whether the summer clothe the general earth
> With greenness, or the redbreast sit and sing
> Betwixt the tufts of snow on the bare branch
> Of mossy apple-tree, while the nighthatch
> Smokes in the sun-thaw; whether the eave-drops fall
> Heard only in the trances of the blast,
> Or if the secret ministry of frost
> Shall hang them up in silent icicles,
> Quietly shining to the quiet Moon.

The stanza, like Keats's *Ode to Autumn*, embraces Nature in her wholeness, integrating fertility and death—the redbreast singing on the bare winter branch—and balancing the peaceful rising motion of the smoke in the "sun-thaw" with the falling of the eave-drops in the "trances of the blast." The final image portrays an unbroken, reciprocal relationship with Nature. Although the icicles have phallic, even destructive, associations, they shine in the benevolent reflection of the moon's light, of the mother's love, and thus the image of the icicles "Quietly shining to the quiet Moon" ultimately projects a true serenity. That equanimity, however, was hard-won. In the manuscript version, Coleridge writes,

> Quietly shining to the quiet moon,
> Like those, my babe! which ere tomorrow's warmth

Have capp'd their sharp keen points with pendulous drops,
Will catch thine eye, and with their novelty
Suspend thy little soul; then make thee shout,
And stretch and flutter from thy mother's arms
As thou wouldst fly for very eagerness.

Here the angry and aggressive feelings toward the mother are still prominent. The icicles have "sharp keen points," and they make the infant shout and fly from its mother's arms. That Coleridge wisely chose to delete these lines, however, suggests an internal reconciliation.

There is far less anger than yearning behind that final image of a mirroring moon/mother. Coleridge prays that his child will experience a reflecting and empathetic relationship with the mother — a relationship that is at the base of identity and of all future human relationships. As Arnold Modell explains, the child's earliest sense of identity, the distinction between I and other, "may be induced by the experience of the child perceiving its mother's face responding to it. The child sees itself reflected in its mother's face."[16] The mirroring moon image occurs elsewhere in Coleridge's poetry and reflects the same longing. In *Limbo* (1817), for instance, Coleridge describes a blind old man who by chance turns his gaze moonward, and

Gazes the orb with moon-like countenance,
With scant white hairs, with foretop bald and high,
He gazes still, — his eyeless face all eye; —
As 'twere an organ full of silent sight,
His whole face seemeth to rejoice in light!
Lip touching lip, all moveless, bust and limb —
He seems to gaze at that which seems to gaze on him!

[24-30]

In *The Nightingale* (1798) Coleridge concludes with a passage that resembles *Frost at Midnight* even more closely. One evening, the poet describes, his infant awoke

In most distressful mood (some inward pain
Had made up that strange thing, an infant's dream —)
I hurried with him to our orchard-plot,
And he beheld the moon, and hushed at once,
Suspends his sobs, and laughs most silently,

While his fair eyes, that swam with undropped tears,
Did glitter in the yellow moon-beam!

[99-105]

Like *Frost at Midnight*, the poem "is a father's tale" (106), and the father concludes with the hope that his child, unlike himself, shall grow up so "that with the night," with the dark, secret realm of the moon, "He may associate joy."

·4·
WORDSWORTH

INTRODUCTION

Wordsworthian criticism has focused increasingly in recent years on the self-doubts and internal conflicts that characterize the poet's relationship with nature. Wordsworth's early faith in nature, his belief in a harmonious interchange between people and nature, is frequently contrasted with his later skepticism and his exaltation of the human mind over nature. The contrast has led the critics to question the strength and depth of that early faith in the first place.[1] As with all of the Romantics, Wordsworth's relationship with nature is essentially ambivalent. Richard Onorato, in *The Character of the Poet: Wordsworth in "The Prelude"* (1971), offers a psychoanalytic interpretation of the poet's complex relationship with nature. Onorato sees the traumatic death of Wordsworth's mother when he was eight years old as the one most formative event in the poet's life and thus as the key to understanding the poetry. According to Onorato, Nature in Wordsworth's poetry always "stands for the protective and feeding mother recollected and desiderated." He stresses the journey metaphor—the search for the lost, ideal mother projected into Nature. "The journey metaphor begins," he asserts, "with the death of the mother and her disappearance from the original vale" (p. 72).

Although Onorato points in an important direction by highlighting the crucial role of the mother, his overall analysis of the poetry as it reflects the personality is ultimately unsatisfactory.

Too much is missing. Some of the most striking dimensions of the personality are ignored—namely, the aggressiveness and destructiveness directed toward Nature or the mother, the consequent guilt, and the compassionate and consciously moral aspect. Wordsworth's poetry expresses less a journey for a lost, ideal mother than a struggle to accept an unideal, human, and imperfect mother and one's own guilt feelings toward her. The motivating force of his poetry is not to recapture the lost mother but to fortify the self in relation to her, to become a power like her, as he hoped *The Prelude* "might become / A power like one of Nature's" (12, 311-12). From this perspective, the loss of the mother at eight would not be the determining psychic trauma; the loss would only reactivate and perhaps intensify an earlier, preestablished trauma. Onorato concentrates solely on loss and aggrievement as the formative feelings of Wordsworth's poetry. Locating the psychic core at an earlier stage, however, in which the operative emotions are ambivalence and guilt, offers a more complete and dynamic view of the personality as it shapes the poetry.

The shortsightedness of Onorato's perspective is perhaps best revealed in his analysis of *Tintern Abbey*. This poem, like *The Prelude*, describes a growth, a maturing self-realization, but, says Onorato, it is a "young man's poem" in which "death is not real" and "change and loss are transformed by Wordsworth's insistence into growth and gain." He believes the poem is essentially regressive, that it expresses the need for a "preferred relationship" with Nature which "precludes a more responsive engagement with other people and places" (p. 79). Drawing on Wordsworth's biography, Onorato describes the poet's "profound experience of the world" and consequent disillusionment in that period between the first visit to the Wye Valley in 1793 and the second visit, in 1798, to *Tintern Abbey*. This leads the critic to assert, "One suspects that Wordsworth was seeking in Nature an object for 'an appetite, a feeling and a love' after having had a dreadful experience of the world of men; also, that what he sought was being projected into Nature and was associated unconsciously . . . with the truly unself-conscious and instinctual gratifications of infancy" (p. 51). Immediately this statement feels wrong. The poem is not expressing a regressive withdrawal from human society: on the contrary, it is reaffirming the relationship of the solitary experience of Nature *with* human community. Furthermore, Nature does not appear in *Tintern Abbey* as the wishful projection of the lost ideal mother.

If the thrust of the poem were essentially regressive, it would be describing a movement toward disintegration and breakdown of self. But the pervasive tone of the poem—serene, assured, deeply and quietly joyful—hardly suggests such underlying instability. Onorato insists, however, that Wordsworth wishes to "lose himself" in the landscape, to withdraw from the world and extinguish his self-consciousness. He feels "that serene and blessed mood" expresses "loss of self" (p. 56). He compares the experience described in that passage, in which "the breath of this corporeal frame / And even the motion of our human blood / Almost suspended, we are laid asleep / In body, and become a living soul," with Wordsworth's account in the Fenwick Notes of a boyhood experience that indeed does express a terrifying threat of disintegration. In the Fenwick Notes Wordsworth describes how as a boy he communed so completely with Nature that he often felt his own nature to be "immaterial" and how "Many times while going to school I grasped at a wall or tree to recall myself from this abyss of idealism to the reality."[2] But Onorato fails to note the profound difference in the emotion informing this experience and that in *Tintern Abbey*. In the former, the feeling is one of terror and deep anxiety (Onorato leaves out the last sentence of the note: "At this time I was afraid of such processes"), whereas in the poem it is one of serenity and "a deep power of joy": "While with an eye made quiet by the power / Of harmony, and the deep power of joy, / We see into the life of things."

The emotional difference is due to the difference in the strength and wholeness of the ego involved in each experience. That "serene and blessed mood" does not describe a *loss* of self in the landscape but the integration of a whole, realized self *with* the environment. Onorato criticizes Wordsworth for regressive and infantile weakness at precisely the point where he is displaying the most strength. The same profound integration is expressed in that other famous passage—

> a sense sublime
> Of something far more deeply interfused,
> Whose dwelling is the light of setting suns,
> And the round ocean and the living air,

And the blue sky, and in the mind of man:
A motion and a spirit, that impels
All thinking things, all objects of all thought,
And rolls through all things.

[95-102]

The self, the "mind of man," is not subsumed or lost in any mystical oneness but participates along with the sun, ocean, air, and sky
in an organic intercommunion.
    Such deep communion with Nature without any accompanying
anxiety over loss of self marks an achievement of the ego. It is a
result of a developing relationship with Nature, the dynamics of
which Onorato does not see. Wordsworth, however, describes it
explicitly:

And so I dare to hope
Though changed, no doubt, from what I was when first
I came among these hills; when like a roe
I bounded o'er the mountains, by the sides
Of the deep rivers, and the lonely streams,
Wherever nature led: more like a man
Flying from something that he dreads than one
Who sought the thing he loved. For nature then
(The coarser pleasures of my boyish days,
And their glad animal movements all gone by)
To me was all in all. —I cannot paint
What then I was. The sounding cataract
Haunted me like a passion: the tall rock,
The mountain, and the deep and gloomy wood,
Their colors and their forms, were then to me
An appetite; a feeling and a love,

. . . .
            —That time is past,
And all its aching joys are now no more,
And all its dizzy raptures.

[64-84]

This passage does not portray Nature as an ideal, protective,
and nourishing maternal presence. The poet describes how he
bounded over the hills like a man "Flying from something that he
dreads." He feels pursued, "haunted"; the "tall rock" and "deep
and gloomy wood" are hardly images of maternal comfort and

security. Onorato misreads this passage and interprets the "Flying from somethat that he dreads" as flying from "thoughts of his recent experience of the world" (p. 36). That line is referring to his first experience in the valley, however, modifying the "I" of "when first / I came among these hills," and therefore before his experience of the world. Wordsworth refers parenthetically to an even earlier experience of Nature—the "glad animal movements all gone by"—but he is concentrating on that essential youthful experience in which Nature was "an appetite," was "all in all." That experience is described as haunting and threatening as well as joyful and rapturous. Finally, the poet emerges from this experience to look on Nature, "Hearing oftentimes / The still, sad music of humanity." Nature thus leads Wordsworth to the human—to a deeply compassionate feeling for human suffering, to a sympathetic relationship with his fellow man. Onorato, failing to see this, admittedly puzzles over the meaning of that "still, sad music of humanity" and its placement in the poem. The line, however, is crucial and reveals the moral influence of Nature which Wordsworth enforces elsewhere in the poem: he owes to Nature those feelings

> Of unremembered pleasure: such, perhaps,
> As have no slight or trivial influence
> On that best portion of a good man's life,
> His little, nameless, unremembered acts
> Of kindness and of love.
>
> [29-34]

And he recognizes in Nature "The guide, the guardian of my heart, and soul / Of all my moral being" (108-11).

Wordsworth's sense of communion with suffering humanity and his powerful feelings of communion and integration with Nature both result from his having passed beyond an earlier experience of Nature. These feelings, he says, are "abundant recompense" for a "loss." He repeatedly tells us how he has changed, that his boyish days of "glad animal movements" are "all gone by," that his experience of Nature as "an appetite," a haunting passion, is "past" and "all its aching joys are now no more." Onorato claims the poem never confronts loss, and by "loss" he means the death of the mother. Clearly, however, the poem does confront a profound loss. It describes the loss of one kind of relationship with Nature or the mother and the development of another. The confrontation with and the acceptance of loss provide both the impetus and the subject of the poem.

Tintern Abbey describes the psychic process involved in the growth of a strong, integrated, and socially oriented, moral self. The process involves the initial loss of a "glad animal" state of being and a consequent "appetite" for Nature with accompanying feelings of being pursued, haunted, threatened. The relationship here is ambivalent, Nature being the source of both dread and joy. Finally, a deep feeling of compassion for one's fellow man develops along with a newly realized sense of self and a powerful feeling of reintegration with Nature. The poem ends on a note of gratitude; the poet feels blessed and he himself blesses Dorothy, providing her with "healing thoughts of tender joy" should she, like himself, ever encounter "solitude, or fear, or pain, or grief."

The process that *Tintern Abbey* describes parallels Endymion's development as he confronts his feelings of loss and ambivalence and is ultimately able to experience gratitude, compassion, and real object love. The "spots of time" in *The Prelude* also express moments of confrontation with unconscious ambivalent emotions. As Jonathon Bishop argues, the spots represent Wordsworth's earliest memories, similar to dreams.[3] Bishop remarks, first of all, on the recurrent nature of these moments: Wordsworth describes them always as experienced "many a time." He also points to the feelings of guilt attached to the spots. Often at the extreme moment of repeated action, the motion is halted, as by the admonishing mountain in the Stolen Boat episode, or by such ghostly figures as the discharged soldier or the drowned man. Finally, the moments usually portray the crossing of a boundary or the breaking of a barrier: the entrance into London, reaching the heights of Snowden, rising out of the water, crossing the Alps. Bishop thus sees these repeated moments of solitary figures crossing barriers as representing, psychologically, moments of transgression. The experiences described by the spots all have a profound significance and power for Wordsworth because of the tremendous force of the libidinal and aggressive feelings involved in the experience. Antisocial impulses or taboo libidinal drives are at the source of the picture of the solitary figure breaking barriers, and thus arise the attendant feelings of guilt, punishment, and retaliation.

The social and moral dimensions of Wordsworth's poetry relate directly to the poet's feelings of guilt, to his need to make repara-

tion for his angry, destructive feelings. The aggression, furthermore, is directed as much toward the father as toward the mother.
The oedipal drama is central to the dynamics of Wordsworth's
poetry. The mother and father figures are clearly differentiated
and, although still the objects of the poet's intensely ambivalent
feelings, they do not disintegrate under the force of those feelings.
While his poems display moments of regression as deep and as
primitive as those in the poetry of Shelley, Keats, or Coleridge, the
narcissistic regression in Wordsworth's work is always halted or
checked by the ego and is submitted to the moral demands of the
social environment. Wordsworth's poetry, in other words, displays
a more fully developed superego and generally a more mature,
integrated self. The vampiric and devouring parental figures, those
sadistic forerunners of the superego, have no place in his poetry.
Furthermore, the most ecstatic moments in his work are not, as
they are in Shelley, Keats, or Byron, moments of self-annihilating
fusion or retreat into an idealized maternal world. Wordsworth's
ecstatic moments express either conquest, as the ascent of Snowden
in *The Prelude*, or a harmonious, integrated relationship with the
environment, as in *Tintern Abbey*. His moments of exultation
display a true liberation, a real resolution of his ambivalent parental ties.

The ascent of Snowden, for instance, expresses both an ascendant independence, a triumphant separation from and power
over the mother, as well as an empathetic alliance, an intimate
collaboration with her. The poet describes, first of all, how he
climbed "With forehead bent / Earthward, as if in opposition set /
Against the enemy" (13, 30-31). He then conveys his jubilation at
reaching the top in the feminine imagery of moon and sea:

> I look'd about, and lo!
> The Moon stood naked in the Heavens, at height
> Immense above my head, and on the shore
> I found myself of a huge sea of mist,
> Which, meek and silent, rested at my feet.
>
> [40-45]

Even further beyond, the poet adds, "the real sea . . . seem'd / To
dwindle, and give up its majesty, / Usurp'd upon," while at the
same time the moon-mother looks benevolently on from "height
immense" above. The moon, in fact, graciously shares in the poet's

conquest: "The moon look'd down upon this shew / In single glory, and we stood, the mist / Touching our very feet; . . ." (52-54). The poet has surmounted his enraged and destructive feelings toward the mother. With the moon above and the mist at his feet, he looks on at a safe distance from the "deep and gloomy" chasm below with its threatening torrential roar.

Wordsworth's confrontation with primeval, ambivalent feelings makes for some of the grandest moments in his poetry. Those "mystical" moments as well as the disturbed, uncanny feelings he so often records are grounded in profound psychic realities; the expansive feelings of communion with Nature express a liberating reconciliation of the poet's ambivalent relations with the mother imago, and the uncanny feelings mark the sudden revelation of repressed unconscious emotions. As Freud explains in "The Uncanny" (1919), "An uncanny experience occurs either when repressed infantile complexes have been revived by some impression, or when the primitive beliefs we have surmounted seem once more to be confirmed." The uncanny is really nothing new or foreign, "but something familiar and old-established in the mind that has been estranged only by the process of repression"—it comes from something repressed which recurs.[4] Freud also discusses the principle of a repetition-compulsion in the unconscious mind and the uncanny effect experienced whenever one is reminded of this inner repetition-compulsion. Freud's analysis illuminates the spots of time, which, as Bishop has pointed out, are usually associated with a repeated action and are described as experienced "many a time." In several of the spots, and in many of the early lyrics, the uncanny experience, the boy/poet's experience of deeply stirring but indescribable emotions, can be traced specifically to the emergence of repressed libidinal and destructive feelings toward the mother imago. As with all of the Romantics, the locus of these ambivalent feelings is the original narcissistic wound—the personality's earliest experience of separation and loss.

AMBIVALENCE AND GUILT
IN THE EARLY POEMS

Of the lyrics composed between 1798 and 1805, a majority concern a mother and a child and revolve around the death or absence of one or the other. Lucy Gray sets out to find her mother in a storm and vanishes in the snow. The idiot boy is sent off by his mother, also on a rescuing errand, to fetch a doctor for the ailing Susan Gale, and he too disappears, only to be found after the mother has experienced much anxiety. Both Lucy and the Winander boy, as favored children of Nature, enjoy a loving communion with it and then abruptly die. *The Affliction of Margaret, Maternal Grief, The Sailor's Mother,* and *The Emigrant Mother* all tell of a mother's grief at the loss of her child. The experience of loss connected with the mother-child relationship lies at the core of much of Wordsworth's poetry. All his lone wanderers and vagrant figures reflect this core experience; cast out from the original home, they must spend their lives in solitary, homeless wandering. One of Wordsworth's earliest poems, *Guilt and Sorrow,* illustrates this connection between the wandering solitary and the original narcissistic wound.

Guilt and Sorrow, or Incidents upon Salisbury Plain presents the story of an old sailor, a suffering wanderer. Yet even in this youthful poem an immediate difference appears between Wordsworth's depiction of the familiar Romantic outcast figure and that of Shelley or Byron. Wordsworth's outcasts never collapse in self-pity, as do Shelley's characters, nor do they die in guilty, bitter despair like many of Byron's heroes. The suffering the characters experience in Wordsworth's poems is almost always regenerative. If his people die, they do so only after they have learned something vital about themselves—usually after they have learned to accept their suffering, their guilt, and learned the meaning and value of compassion. *Guilt and Sorrow* opens with a portrait of the tattered and weary sailor pursuing his "vagrant way" across a lonely plain:

> Long had he fancied each successive slope
> Concealed some cottage, whither he might turn
> And rest; but now along heaven's darkening cope
> The crows rushed by in eddies, homeward borne.
> Thus warned he sought some shepherd's spreading thorn
> Or hovel from the storm to shield his head,
> But sought in vain; for now, all wild, forlorn,
> And vacant, a huge waste around him spread;
> The wet cold ground, he feared must be his only bed.
>
> [37-45]

Unlike Shelley's homeless heroes, however, Wordsworth's forlorn traveler feels responsible for his bereft condition. Unable to
provide his family with "their needful food," he robbed and mur-
dered a man, "And when the miserable work was done / He fled, a
vagrant since, the murderer's fate to shun" (72-73). The landscape,
"dark and void as ocean's watery realm," reflects the condition of
his own blackened soul. The poem is a strong indictment of the
social conditions of the time; nevertheless, the passion with which
the poet attacks the prevailing poverty and hunger derives strength
from the personality's deep, unconscious feelings of deprivation
and frustration. At one point in the poem, the sailor encounters a
distraught woman who is weeping over her wounded child. The
child "had provoked his father" who then beat him. In *The Music
of Humanity*, Jonathan Wordsworth provides an earlier version of
the passage which betrays the oral roots of the conflict. The woman
is sitting "Near an old mat with broken bread bestrown"—the
scene was set for breakfast: "Her husband for that pitcher rose; his
place / The infant took, . . . / And when desired to move, with
smiling face / For a short while did in obedience fail" (p. 57).

The husband then furiously beats the child. The oedipal dynamics are obvious. When the sailor sees the battered child, he
groans "As if he saw—there upon that ground— / Strange repetition of the deadly wound / He had himself inflicted" (489-92). The
sailor thus identifies with the husband who was thwarted in his
efforts to secure the pitcher—a symbol of oral gratification. His
envy and frustration lead to the violent outburst of enraged aggression.

The narcissistic wound—the feeling of maternal deprivation
and loss—is at the heart of Wordsworth's guilty and depressed
vagrant figures. He always associates loss and sorrow with guilt.
His work reflects a personality that, in Winnicott's terms, has
reached the "stage of concern"; the self has accepted responsibility
for its enraged and aggressive feelings over that original experience
of loss. The psychic dynamics of *Guilt and Sorrow* also inform the
spots of time in *The Prelude*. The Beacon spot, for instance, distinctly echoes a moment in the earlier poem. As the sailor plods
along at the beginning of *Guilt and Sorrow*, he hears the "sullen
clang of chains": "He looked, and saw upon a gibbet high / A
human body that in irons swang, / Uplifted by the tempest whirl-
ing by; / And, hovering, round it often did a raven fly" (76-81).

The spectacle "roused a train / Of the mind's phantoms" and the sailor falls in a motionless trance. Wordsworth remarks on the "rage" of the elements and describes how a lone bustard "forced hard against the wind a thick unwieldy flight" (108). In Book 11 of *The Prelude*, Wordsworth describes how once, as a boy, while riding in the hills, he became separated from his companion and accidently stumbled upon a gibbet-mast "where in former times / A murderer had been hung in iron chains" (290). Although the bones and iron case are gone, the boy sees the murderer's name carved indelibly in the ground. Wordsworth continues,

> . . . forthwith I left the spot
> And, reascending the bare Common, saw
> A naked Pool that lay beneath the hills,
> The Beacon on the summit, and more near,
> A Girl who bore a Pitcher on her head
> And seem'd with difficult steps to force her way
> Against the blowing wind. It was, in truth,
> An ordinary sight; but I should need
> Colours and words that are unknown to man
> To paint the visionary dreariness
> Which, while I look'd all round for my lost guide,
> Did at that time invest the naked Pool,
> The Beacon on the lonely Eminence,
> The Woman, and her garments vex'd and toss'd
> By the Strong wind.
>
> [302-16]

Onorato sees this spot as a crucial screen memory, invested with memories of the mother. The vision concerns, he believes, Wordsworth's feelings of despair and inadequacy over his mother's death. Yet Onorato again overlooks the equally intense feelings of murderous rage and guilt which also surround the incident. The vision significantly follows the troubled thoughts about the murderer. Just as the sailor's murder in *Guilt and Sorrow* stems, at bottom, from a frustrated maternal relationship, so the boy's sight of the gibbet-mast is intimately associated with the vision of the pool, the beacon, and the girl which follows; the murderous associations indeed account for the impact of the scene. Both the "naked Pool" and the "Girl who bore a Pitcher on her head" have maternal associations (the pitcher here may be considered a displaced breast symbol). The "Beacon on the lonely Eminence" suggests a vigilant paternal presence. The vision occurs, furthermore, after the boy has significantly become *separated* from his guide; the "visionary dreariness" descended, he repeats, "while I look'd all round for my lost guide." The experience of separation and loss is thus again at the root of the murderous thoughts surrounding the mother. The enraged feelings toward the mother are betrayed further in the image of the girl "vex'd and toss'd" by the storm. Like the lone bustard in *Guilt and Sorrow*, the girl must "force her way" against an angry, blowing wind. The depth and force of the conflicting unconscious emotions informing the scene account for the powerful influence that it exerts over the boy.

Water images, like the naked pool in the beacon spot, figure prominently in many of the spots and in Wordsworth's poetry generally. The lakes, streams, seas, and waterfalls that enliven his landscapes are always the agents of either deep joy or of profound terror and destruction. The water images, again, are associated with the mother imago. Wordsworth refers frequently to the "bosom of the lake" or pool and to the "breast of open seas." Water is invested with a distinct "power" and often with a loud, chastising, or threatening "voice." In the climb up Snowden, for instance, the poet's feeling of ascendant power is imaged in his commanding the sea at his feet, while further off the "roar of waters, torrents, streams / Innumerable, roaring with one voice" sounds a more distant threat. At the Simplon Pass, the "stationary blasts of water-falls" contributes to the mighty apocalyptic vision and the poet describes being "deafen'd and stunn'd / By noise of waters" (6, 578-79). The ghastly figure of the drowned man rises up out of a "calm Lake" which "Grew dark, with all the shadows on its breast" (5, 464). For the Winander boy, the "voice of mountain-torrents" carries "a gentle shock of mild surprise" while

> . . . the visible scene
> Would enter unawares into his mind
> With all its solemn imagery, its rocks,
> Its woods, and that uncertain heaven received
> Into the bosom of the steady lake.
>
> ["There Was a Boy," 19-25]

The water image, like the mother imago, is a nourishing, receiving, comforting presence while also the source of a terrifying vengeance, of a fearful "dark ministry."

The Prelude book on the poet's childhood contains three other spots that also revolve around the boy/poet's ambivalent feelings toward the mother imago. Just as the sailor in "Guilt and Sorrow" robs and murders, so the boy Wordsworth commits acts of theft and destruction, and those acts account for some of his most moving and disturbing experiences. He describes himself, for instance, as a "plunderer" of the nests the "Mother bird had built." He "hung alone," he says, above a "perilous ridge" while "With what strange utterance did the loud dry wind / Blow through my ears! the sky seem'd not a sky / Of earth, and with what motion mov'd the clouds!" (1, 347-50). The loud wind suggests, as usual, an angry, retaliating, and chastising Nature, but here the boy triumphs in his illicit act. His survival of both his own destructive impulses and the mother's retaliation gives rise to the exhilarated feelings. In the stolen boat episode, however, Nature's retaliatory power is stronger and leaves the boy more profoundly disturbed. The incident again concerns "an act of stealth / And troubled pleasure" (1, 388-89). The illicit and destructive feelings are apparent in Wordsworth's description: "lustily," he says, "I dipp'd my oars into the silent Lake," and when the huge cliff "uprais'd its head" and seemed to stride after him, "I struck, and struck again." (408). The boy finally steals his way "Back to the Cavern of the Willow tree," and for many days after, he says, "in my thoughts / There was a darkness, call it solitude, / Or blank desertion," a sense of "huge and mighty Forms" which "mov'd slowly through my mind / By day and were the trouble of my dreams" (421-27). The incident, as an externalization of the boy's ambivalent relations with the parent imagos (the cliffs suggest a paternal as well as maternal retaliation), results in the deep sense of inner disruption with which he concludes.

The skating spot reveals the same emotional dynamics, only here the boy prevails over the retaliatory cliffs, and thus, rather than dark thoughts and troubled dreams, he experiences a tranquility like "a dreamless sleep." Wordsworth's description again betrays the antisocial and essentially destructive nature of the act. He describes how he often "retired / Into a silent bay," separated himself from the crowd, "To cut across the image of a star / That gleam'd upon the ice." While spinning on the ice, he says, "the shadowy banks, on either side, / Came sweeping through the darkness" in a wild and rapid motion, much like the clouds in the bird nest spot. He would then, however, stop short.

> ... yet still the solitary Cliffs
> Wheeled by me, even as if the earth had roll'd
> With visible motion her diurnal round;
> Behind me did they stretch in solemn train
> Feebler and feebler, and I stood and watch'd
> Till all was tranquil as a dreamless sleep
>
> [1, 484-49]

The cliffs significantly stretch "behind" him, "Feebler and feebler." As in the Snowden climb, the boy/poet's ability to withstand, to triumph over, the destructiveness in his relations with the parent imagos ultimately results in his deep sense of inner tranquility.

Several of the early lyrics are constructed on these same ambivalent relationships and they conclude, like the stolen boat episode, with a painful, troubling sense of guilt. In *Nutting* (1798), for instance, the boy Wordsworth sets out alone on a nutting expedition, and after "Forcing" his way "Through beds of matted fern, and tangled thickets," he comes upon an untouched nook, "A virgin scene!"

> ... —A little while I stood,
> Breathing with such suppression of the heart
> As joy delights in; and with wise restraint
> Voluptuous, fearless of a rival, eyed
> The banquet;— ...
>
> [21-25]

The description betrays a primitive oral greed as well as oedipal feelings toward the mother. The poet continues to describe his indulgence in the pleasures of the spot, as

> The heart luxuriates with indifferent things,
> Wasting its kindliness on stocks and stones,
> And on the vacant air. Then up I rose,
> And dragged to earth both branch and bough, with crash
> And merciless ravage: and the shady nook
> Of hazels, and the green and mossy bower,

Deformed and sullied, patiently gave up
Their quiet being . . .

[41-48]

The enraged violence the boy suddenly turns on Nature relates
back to those "indifferent" and "vacant" qualities he ascribes to it
at first. Again, the boy projects his own fears and guilt over his destructiveness back onto the natural scene:

. . . and unless I now
Confound my present feelings with the past,
Ere from the mutilated bower I turned
Exulting, rich beyond the wealth of kings,
I felt a sense of pain when I beheld
The silent trees, and saw the intruding sky.—

[48-53]

A Night-Piece (1798) also portrays illicit and disturbing feelings toward the mother imago. Wordsworth describes a sky over-
cast with clouds that "veil" an indistinct and "dull" moon. A
pensive, lonesome traveler making his way beneath this sky is at
once startled by an "instantaneous gleam."

. . . he looks up—the clouds are split
Asunder,—and above his head he sees
The clear Moon, and the glory of the heavens.
There in a black-blue vault she sails along,
Followed by multitudes of stars, that, small
And sharp, and bright, along the dark abyss
Drive as she drives: how fast they wheel away,
Yet vanish not! . . .
. . . and the vault,
Built round by those white clouds, enormous clouds,
Still deepens its unfathomable depth.

[10-22]

The scene is invested with feelings that are both destructive and
frightening. The clouds do not simply part but are "split asunder";
the traveler's access to the vision is a violent one. The moon,
furthermore, sails along in a "dark abyss" and exerts a powerful
driving force—she drives the stars away. The vault of the "enor-

mous clouds," which the traveler's eye has now penetrated, "Still deepens its unfathomable depth," as if promising even greater obscurity. Wordsworth concludes: "At length the Vision closes; and the mind, / Not undisturbed by the delight it feels, / Which slowly settles into peaceful calm, / Is left to muse upon the solemn scene." The delight in violating the mysterious feminine realm is accompanied, as usual in Wordsworth's poetry, by disturbed and sobering thoughts.

Finally, Wordsworth's ambivalent feelings toward the mother imago also underlie the "Lucy" poems. Upon examining the unconscious emotions beneath the surface of these deceptively simple lyrics, one discovers some unsuspected dimensions. Of the several "Lucy" poems, *Strange fits of passion* is perhaps the most complex:

> Strange fits of passion have I known:
> And I will dare to tell,
> But in the Lover's ear alone,
> What once to me befell.
>
> When she I loved looked every day
> Fresh as a rose in June,
> I to her cottage bent my way,
> Beneath an evening-moon.

The parallel motion of the sinking moon and the thoughts and movements of the Lover as he, too, bends his way down to the cottage has been commonly recognized. For the reader, when the moon finally drops behind the cot, the association with the thought of Lucy's death seems natural; one feels prepared for that connection. For the speaker, however, that association does not seem a natural one at all: "What fond and wayward thoughts will slide / Into a Lover's head!" he cries. Furthermore, he is appalled and terrified when he actually does make the connection. He describes the episode as a "strange fit of passion." The lover experiences the parallel vision of the sinking moon and Lucy's death as wayward and strange precisely because it expresses a repressed and "wayward" unconscious wish. The lover's ambivalence makes for the intensity of response at the end.

The speaker, first of all, obviously feels both guilty and fearful. Why else would he only "dare to tell / But in the Lover's ear alone / What once to me befell"? Only another lover, perhaps, could understand the darker emotions on the underside of love. The movement of the speaker in the poem, furthermore, is not only allied with that of the moon, but actually seems to spur it on, to encourage its descent. The lover "fixed" his eye on the moon and then "With quickening pace my horse drew nigh" as the moon sinks "near, and nearer still" Lucy's cot. Then, with eyes "all the while . . . kept / On the descending moon," the lover curiously remarks how he slept "In one of those sweet dreams." The thoughts of the sinking moon/dying woman thus give rise to a regressive, pleasurable experience. The lover's horse keeps moving, "hoof after hoof / He raised and never stopped" until the moon actually drops and the lover, suddenly terrified lest his destructive fantasy prove real, cries, "'O mercy! . . . / If Lucy should be dead!'"

Whereas *Strange fits of passion* reveals the poet's ambivalent feelings toward the image of the woman, *Three years she grew in sun and shower* portrays Nature or the Mother as the ambivalent lover.

> Three years she grew in sun and shower,
> Then Nature said, "A lovelier flower
> On earth was never sown;
> This Child I to myself will take;
> She shall be mine, and I will make
> A Lady of my own."

At first Nature's possession of the child is made to seem quite privileged and desirable. The mother promises that the child "Shall feel an overseeing power" (11), and that "she shall lean her ear / In many a secret place" (26-27). Yet although she "shall be sportive as the fawn," hers is also "the silence and the calm / Of mute insensate things" (16-17), and it is to this mute and deadly calm that the poet returns at the end:

> Thus Nature spake—The work was done—
> How soon my Lucy's race was run!
> She died, and left to me
> This heath, this calm, and quiet scene;
> The memory of what has been,
> And never more will be.

Nature's love also means death. In *There Was a Boy*, the Winander boy also enjoys a favored relationship with Nature, yet that poem too ends with the poet standing "Mute—looking at the grave in which he lies." Both poems are elegies for a lost infant self and for a lost union with the mother. The yearned-for fusion with the mother, however, must inevitably result in death. The poet's ambivalent feelings over that union are even more apparent in *A slumber did my spirit seal*:

> A slumber did my spirit seal;
>   I had no human fears:
> She seemed a thing that could not feel
>   The touch of earthly years.
>
> No motion has she now, no force;
>   She neither hears nor sees,
> Rolled round in earth's diurnal course,
>   With rocks, and stones, and trees.

Critics have debated endlessly over the poet's attitude in this lyric. Is Lucy's rolling round with the rocks and stones and trees a joyous or melancholy event? Surely all the negatives—"no motion," "no force," "neither hears nor sees"—suggest some regret. Yet that cyclical harmony and communion with Nature is always invested with joy in Wordsworth's poetry. The resonating strength of the lyric is perhaps derived from the very tension of the ambivalence itself.

Like the "Lucy" poems, all of Wordsworth's elegies center around the original narcissistic loss. The greatest of these elegies, *Elegaic Stanzas, Suggested by a Picture of Peele Castle*, and *Ode: Intimations of Immortality from Recollections of Early Childhood*, do not simply mourn the loss, they confront and present a resolution of it. The poems chronicle the psychic movement through loss of the original oneness or fusion with the mother to a confrontation with intensely ambivalent feelings and finally to an acceptance of separateness and aloneness and to a reconciliation with reality. An examination of the psychodynamics of these two poems can prepare for an understanding of the most characteristic female image in Wordsworth's poetry—the abandoned woman.

THE ELEGIES:
PEELE CASTLE AND THE *ODE*

The same experience of profound loss at the heart of *Tintern Abbey*, *Guilt and Sorrow*, and the "Lucy" poems also forms the core of the *Intimations Ode* (1803) and *Elegaic Stanzas, Suggested by a Picture of Peele Castle* (1805). Although the *Ode* was composed before *Peele Castle*, the latter poem presents a simpler, more direct expression of that loss and thus provides a good preface to a critical understanding of the *Ode*. *Peele Castle* refers to a specific loss—the death of Wordsworth's brother John in 1805. The actual loss, however, only repeats and reactivates the deeper psychic loss. The poem begins, as does *Tintern Abbey*, by recalling a past relationship: "I was thy neighbor once, thou rugged Pile! / Four summer weeks I dwelt in sight of thee: / I saw thee every day; and all the while / Thy Form was sleeping on a glassy sea." As Wordsworth goes on to describe the scene, he emphasizes its "sleeping," still quality, its absolute peace and calm. Not only is the sea "glassy" but the sky is "pure," the air "so quiet," the calm "perfect," and the "mighty Deep / Was even the gentlest of all gentle things." In these first few stanzas, Wordsworth also stresses the perfect stasis of the scene and its inviolability. Each day was "so like, so very like," and the castle's "Image" is always there; it "never passed away." The calm is so perfect that "it seemed no sleep; / No mood, which season takes away, or brings." Wordsworth continues to emphasize these qualities as he describes how he would have painted the scene "if mine had been the Painter's hand." He would have placed the castle "Beside a sea that could not cease to smile," the picture would have been "of lasting ease, / Elysian quiet, without toil or strife; / No motion but the moving tide," and finally, he exclaims, "Such, in the fond illusion of my heart, / Such Picture would I at that time have made: / And seen the soul of truth in every part, / A steadfast peace that might not be betrayed."

Such a picture suggests the perfect harmony, peace, and stasis of existence inside the womb. It suggests too the infantile wish for an ever-present, ever-smiling, purely benevolent, good mother. The words *steadfast* and *betrayed* in the above stanza are the clues to the real emotional crux of the poem. The poet yearns for a fulfillment, for a peace that is "steadfast" and that "might not be

betrayed" only because that fulfillment has not been perfect, because the peace has been broken, and he has felt betrayed. The
first half of the poem describes the bliss of prenatal existence, a
bliss that is necessarily shattered at birth as one enters into "aloneness" and into relationship with a human and imperfect mother.
The poem leads to the belief that the poet once actually lived such
an Elysian existence, but that is surely impossible, especially if one
considers Wordsworth's account of his childhood and youth in
The Prelude. Furthermore, Wordsworth describes how, had he
painted the picture, he would have added "the gleam, / The light
that never was, on sea or land, / The consecration, and the Poet's
dream." The light never actually was there, only imagined; the
gleam is a product of the poetic imagination, of "the Poet's dream."
The blissful, harmonic existence the first half of the poem describes, then, is more an imaginatively realized intuition, a sensed
recollection of a past psychic state rather than an actual one. One
is thus prepared for the following stanza, which is the turning
point of the poem and a critical passage in relation to the whole of
Wordsworth's work: "So once it would have been,—'tis so no
more; / I have submitted to a new control: / A power is gone,
which nothing can restore; / A deep distress hath humanised my
Soul."

No critic has, to my mind, satisfactorily explained these lines.
Why should a "deep distress" necessarily "humanise" his soul, and
what exactly is the "power" that is gone? Relating this passage to
the *Immortality Ode*, to which it is closely tied, some critics have
identified this power with Wordsworth's poetic powers, which he
feels he has lost. Trilling, on the other hand, rightly discredits this
interpretation but then relates this power to a way of "seeing" and
imagining, to a youthful mode of perception—"fancy," dreams,
and illusions—which the poet has now passed beyond.[5] Clearly,
however, this power relates to something deeper and more encompassing than a way of seeing; it refers to a way of being, to
that blissful Elysian existence described in the first half of the
poem. It is the blissful existence of "the Infant Babe" in Book 2 of
The Prelude:

>   . . . Bless'd the infant Babe,
> (For with my best conjectures I would trace
> The progress of our being) blest the Babe,

Nurs'd in his Mother's arms, the Babe who sleeps
Upon his Mother's breast, who, when his soul
Claims manifest kindred with an earthly soul,
Doth gather passion from his Mother's eye!
Such feelings pass into his torpid life
Like an awakening breeze, and hence his mind
Even in the first trial of its powers
Is prompt and watchful, eager to combine
In one appearance, all the elements
And parts of the same object, else detach'd
And loth to coalesce. Thus, day by day,
Subjected to the discipline of love,
His organs and recipient faculties
Are quickened, are more vigorous, his mind spreads,
Tenacious of the forms which it receives.
. . . .
No outcast he, bewilder'd and depress'd;
Along his infant veins are interfus'd
The gravitation and the filial bond
Of nature, that connect him with the world.

[233-64, 1805]

Wordsworth is here intuitively recognizing that the infantile experience of the mother is the first experience of reality and that the dynamics of this relationship form the basis of one's entire experience of the world. The infant first realizes or identifies itself in relation to its mother; the loving gleam in the mother's eye reflects, as it were, the infant's being and confirms its sense of its own reality. So Wordsworth writes of the babe who first realizes himself "when his soul / Claims manifest kindred with an earthly soul," as he gathers "passion from his Mother's eye!" Wordsworth then describes how this passion, the feelings of love the mother projects, "pass into his torpid life / Like an awakening breeze" and prompt the infant "to combine," "to coalesce" all objects in its world into "one appearance." Maternal love, this "filial bond of nature," is thus the source of all love, of all feelings of unity and connection with the world. This is precisely what Harry Guntrip describes as the psychic core of human experience: "The deepest thing in human experience is 'togetherness.' From that starting point the psyche passes through the separation of birth into 'aloneness,' which would be intolerable unless beneath it, as its foundation, there still persisted that oneness of the child with the mother, and through her with 'mother-nature.'"[6]

Thus, the lost "power," which Wordsworth laments in *Peele Castle*, is the benevolent maternal power that he feels he was originally at one with, a power that was originally "interfus'd" along his "infant veins." Wordsworth always describes Nature as a "power" and his poetry is, above all, about power relationships. He continually describes the painful emergence from an initial identification with maternal omnipotence to a confrontation with one's deeply ambivalent feelings toward the powerful mother, and finally to a realization of one's own separate and independent power.

In *Peele Castle* the power related to an original identification with a benevolent mother is gone and replaced by a deep and humanizing distress. The distress or depression is a result of the painful acceptance of loss and separateness and of one's angry and destructive feelings. This acceptance marks an achievement, a maturation, in the personality and thus the "distress" ultimately has a strengthening, calming effect. The poet knows he has "submitted to a new control" and can express his loss with tranquil assurance: "Not for a moment could I now behold / A smiling sea, and be what I have been: / The feeling of my loss will ne'er be old; / this, which I know, I speak with mind serene."

In the three stanzas that follow, Wordsworth describes the violent and destructive nature of Beaumont's scene and commends the painter for the truthfulness of his portrayal. The sea is now "in anger," the shore "dismal," the sky "rueful" and the whole a "pageantry of fear." The poet is able to confront his enraged feelings that he projects onto the natural scene. Amidst all the "deadly swell," the castle stands "sublime" and "braves" the "lightning, the fierce wind, and trampling waves." As a symbolic image of the mother, the castle staunchly withstands the poet's angry and violent feelings. Neither the mother nor the self, in other words, is destroyed, and this uplifts and fortifies the poet. His confrontation with aggressive and destructive feelings ultimately humanizes him, for it leads to an actively reparative, socially integrative and moral attitude. Wordsworth recognizes the regressive withdrawal inherent in that earlier state of bliss: "Farewell, farewell the heart that lives alone, / Housed in a dream, at distance from the Kind! / Such happiness, wherever it be known, / Is to be pitied; for 'tis surely blind."

In the final stanza he thus welcomes "fortitude and patient cheer," the products of his distress. Through his depression, Wordsworth has discovered a new faith—a faith in the human capacity to withstand and endure painful reality and faith in the possibilities for "real" loving relationships: "But welcome fortitude and patient cheer, / And frequent sights of what is to be borne! / Such sights, or worse, as are before me here.— / Not without hope we suffer and we mourn."

The *Intimations Ode* is essentially another version of the same emotional tensions and psychic dynamics that inform *Peele Castle*. The first four stanzas lament the loss of the blissful existence described in the latter poem. There was a time, the poet says, in which all the earth "did seem / Apparelled in celestial light, / The glory and the freshness of a dream," the same "light" of the "Poet's dream" in *Peele Castle*. Wordsworth describes this former existence as one of perfect harmony and reciprocity, of simple, pure delight:

> The Rainbow comes and goes,
> And lovely is the Rose,
> The moon doth with delight
> Look round her when the heavens are bare,
> Waters on a starry night
> Are beautiful and fair;
> . . . .

But the first four stanzas all lead to the obsessing question, the tension that motivates the poem—"Where is it now, the glory and the dream?" (57).

In stanzas 5 and 6 Wordsworth attempts an explanation, harkening back as usual to birth and infancy for the answers. He uses the metaphor of heavenly preexistence: "Our birth is but a sleep and a forgetting," our soul "hath had elsewhere its setting," we come into the world "trailing clouds of glory," and "Heaven lies about us in our infancy!" Both "light" and "joy," the light and joy of the first four stanzas, are now explicitly associated with that "heaven" of infancy. As people grow old, however, their vision of this joyous light dims: "At length the Man perceives it die away, / And fade into the light of common day." Trilling's influential essay on the *Ode* has done much to discourage "mystical" or theistical readings of the poem and has focused attention where it belongs—on the naturalistic, on the common human experience that the *Ode* is describing. The notion of heavenly preexistence, Trilling says, is a "conceit" intended to express the natural experience of prenatality and "of the infant's state of feeling before he has learned to distinguish between the stimuli of his own sensations and those of the world outside." He refers to Freud's discussion of the "oceanic" sensation of "being at one with the universe," which is essentially the same thing as Guntrip's "togetherness." Trilling says the *Ode* is about "growing up," about leaving one stage of being and entering another, about "the development of the sense of reality" (p. 163).

In his actual interpretation of the *Ode*, however, Trilling does not let this perspective carry him far enough. He parts from it too quickly to talk about "optics" and "epistomology." The psychological process of growth that the *Ode* describes is more continuous than Trilling allows. By discussing the blissful union of the prenatal experience as a mode of seeing and knowing rather than being, he forces a disjunction in Wordsworth's vision which is not really there. That union, Trilling says, is a way of "seeing the universe fitted to the mind and the mind to the universe," which leads him to assert that Wordsworth "bestows upon man a dignity which cannot be derived from looking at him in the actualities of common life, from seeing him engaged in business, in morality and politics." Thus, Trilling maintains, Wordsworth has a "double vision": man is "conceived of as 'imperial'" and as he "actually is in the field of life," in his "ideal nature" and in his "earthly activity," and that the relation of man to his fellows in the moral world of difficulty and pain "grows up beside" the relation of man to Nature (p. 165). This is simply not true; the relationships are one and continuous, the one grows out of the other, and Wordsworth indeed does see dignity in people as they actually are in common life—it is, in fact, his constant theme.

Much of Trilling's argument is based on a crucial misinterpretation of stanza 6. This stanza is essentially a continuation of the thought which concludes stanza 5, that the memory of that glorious "light" of infancy must fade with age:

> Earth fills her lap with pleasures of her own;
> Yearnings she hath in her own natural kind,
> And, even with something of a Mother's mind,
>   And no unworthy aim,
> The homely Nurse doth all she can

To make her Foster-child, her Inmate Man,
  Forget the glories he hath known
And that imperial palace whence he came.

Trilling makes a distinction between "Earth" and "Nature," and equates "Earth" here with "World." The Earth is then a second mother, a foster mother, while the true mother is Nature—thus the "double vision." But "earth" is, in fact, used synonymously, or at least in conjunction with, Nature in the first four stanzas ("There was a time when meadow, grove, and stream, / The earth, and every common sight," or "And all the earth is gay"). Stanza 6 is really expressing the poet's maturing sense of Earth-Nature-Mother as a whole and separate identity apart from the self—as one having "pleasures of her own" and "yearnings . . . in her own natural kind." Such a realization implies a sense of one's own separate identity and definition which must necessarily diminish that past sense of glory, of infinite extension and oneness. It is the Mother's intent, Wordsworth says, to make the child "forget" these past glories, but it is "no unworthy aim," for only by relinquishing these past glories can the child achieve a wholeness and identity of its own.

   Nevertheless, this sense of past glory, this joyous togetherness at the source of our being, Wordsworth says, is the "heritage" of the child and "is not to be put by." We yet remember "What was so fugitive," and in stanza 9 Wordsworth gives thanks for these remembrances: "the thought of our past years in me doth breed / Perpetual benediction." However, he gives thanks "not indeed / For that which is most worthy to be blest; / Delight and liberty," the blessings which he celebrates and mourns in the first four stanzas, but for

              . . . those obstinate questionings
        Of sense and outward things,
        Fallings from us, vanishings;
           Blank misgivings of a Creature
        Moving about in worlds not realised,
        High instincts before which our mortal Nature
        Did tremble like a guilty thing surprised:
              But for those first affections,
           Those shadowy recollections,

> Which, be they what they may,
> Are yet the fountain-light of all our day,
> . . . .

[145-55]

Trilling equates these "vanishings" with the "glory" and "light" of stanza 5, but clearly Wordsworth is now refering to something else. The "blank misgivings," the trembling "like a guilty thing surprised," and the "shadowy recollections" all suggest something quite different from the glowing splendor and bliss described earlier. Here once again Wordsworth's ambivalent feelings are made evident. This passage provides the clues, in fact, to understanding that moral influence Nature has for Wordsworth. He is giving thanks for those darker recollections, for those past moments of pain and terror such as chronicled in the spots of time. Such confrontations with his own inner hostility, rage, and destructiveness shock and overwhelm him with guilt. These moments, these past meetings with terror and guilt, however, are the real "fountain light of all our days." Thus, that "immortal sea / Which brought us hither" exerts a dual influence; it leaves us with a sense of past glory and oneness and, most importantly, it chastens and subdues and is the guide and guardian of our moral being. Wordsworth's intimations of that "immortal sea," his intimations of those earliest relationships with the mother, finally have a bracing, invigorating effect—he is able to find strength in the "primal sympathy / Which having been must ever be," and "In the soothing thoughts that spring / Out of human suffering," in human endurance and fortitude, "In the faith that looks through death, / In years that bring the philosophic mind." The final lines of the *Ode* express a mature acceptance and gratitude: "Thanks to the human heart by which we live, / Thanks to its tenderness, its joys, and fears, / To me the meanest flower that blows can give / Thoughts that do often lie too deep for tears." The "meanest flower" can arouse thoughts that are deeper than tears of sorrow and loss, more profound than tears of pity—thoughts of the human fortitude, dignity, and compassion that can spring only from suffering.

Both *Peele Castle* and the *Ode* chronicle a maturation in the poet's personality; they trace an integration and resolution of the personality's ambivalent relations with the mother imago. Wordsworth's image of the suffering and forsaken woman reflects the same psychodynamics. His abandoned women reveal both his ambivalent feelings as well as his resolution of those feelings. The women are victims but, more importantly, also survivors of the poet's deep, destructive rage. They do not dissolve, as do Shelley's women, under the force of the poet's anger. Contrarily, they exhibit an inviolable reality, a concrete solidity, a singular capacity for endurance and courage. As Wordsworth learns in the *Ode* to accept the mother as a whole reality, so the images of women throughout his poetry reflect that wholeness. The abandoned women embody that compassion, fortitude, and dignity Wordsworth has come to understand at the end of the *Ode*.

THE IMAGE OF
THE ABANDONED WOMAN

A prototype for Wordsworth's most characteristic image of the woman has already appeared in the discussion of *Peele Castle*. The picture of the castle standing "sublime," as it "braves" the "lightning, the fierce wind, and trampling waves" typifies the Wordsworthian portrait of the suffering but stoic woman, isolated, in a hostile and aggressive environment. The woman with the pitcher on her head in the beacon "spot," for instance, also patiently forces her way against a violent wind. The image, far from arousing feelings of despair and inadequacy, as Onorato maintains, calls forth in the poet's memory a "spirit of pleasure," a "radiance" divine, and a "power" (11, 323-25). The feeling is similar to that expressed in *The Solitary Reaper* (1805). Here again the woman stands "single" in the field—a "solitary Highland Lass!" Although she is not battling directly against an aggressive Nature, she is singing a "melancholy strain," that tells, the poet believes, of "battles long ago," of "Some natural sorrow, loss, or pain, / That has been, and may be again." Her steady, uninterrupted work in the field suggests the same stalwart endurance as that of the girl with the pitcher, forcing her way through the storm. It is this very quality of endurance which has such a moving and bracing effect on the poet. *The Solitary Reaper* concludes,

> Whate'er the theme, the Maiden sang
> As if her song could have no ending;

> I saw her singing at her work,
> And o'er the sickle bending;—
> I listened, motionless and still;
> And, as I mounted up the hill,
> The music in my heart I bore,
> Long after it was heard no more.

The poet stresses that the maiden sang "As if her song could have no ending" and even the present participial verbs—"singing" and "bending"—suggest a continuous, never-ending quality. This sense of the woman's eternal vitality, of her indestructible reality, deeply moves and uplifts the poet—he mounts the hill bearing her music securely in his heart. Wordsworth is always profoundly heartened by the image of the woman as enduring and inviolable for it suggests that she is able to withstand his own deeply destructive feelings. In psychoanalytic terms, it reflects the capacity of the "good" mother imago to remain intact despite the violence of the infantile rage and aggression directed toward it. This ability to keep the woman whole, to allow her her single, separate reality, marks an achievement in the personality and is thus accompanied by feelings of comfort and deep joy and by a renewed faith in the self.

Wordsworth's abandoned women thus again reflect that core experience of loss and rage in the early mother-child relationship. The women are made to suffer, perhaps as punishment, the same loss and abandonment that the child/poet himself has experienced. Their condition, however, ultimately reflects less aggression than compassion, for to allow the woman to suffer is to grant her her humanity (much as Keats's achievement in *The Fall* is to see the goddess as both humanly suffering and compassionate). Thus, the image of the forsaken woman in a hostile environment at once splits and yet integrates the maternal image, expressing both Wordsworth's ambivalent feelings and his resolution of them. Whereas *The Solitary Reaper* manages to distance that ambivalent experience (the poet sees the maiden from afar and cannot even hear the actual words of her song) and to treat it with a controlled economy, *The Ruined Cottage*, Wordsworth's first attempt to deal fully with the experience, remains closer to the threatening, disruptive emotions. The poem portrays, even more effectively than the later *Ode*, the personality's struggle to accept its feelings of loss and ambivalence. Of all the abandoned women, Margaret most powerfully embodies Wordsworth's ultimate faith in the strength and endurance of the woman's love.

THE RUINED COTTAGE:
MARGARET'S HUMANIZING DISTRESS

First written in 1797-98, *The Ruined Cottage* went through numerous revisions before it finally appeared as Book 1 of *The Excursion* in 1814. Even as late as 1845, however, important changes were still being made. I believe, along with Jonathan Wordsworth, that *The Ruined Cottage*, in its original form, is Wordsworth's first great poem, and I will refer in my analysis of it to the text that Jonathan Wordsworth provides in his critical study *The Music of Humanity.*[7] The first version of the poem, dating from May/June 1797, focuses solely on the tragic story of Margaret, without the character study of the pedlar who narrates the tale. Although the life history of the pedlar, added later in 1798, is intimately related to the Margaret story, I agree with Jonathan Wordsworth that the two parts can be considered in isolation, and it is on the portrait of Margaret that I will focus.

From his study of the manuscript drafts of the poem, Jonathan Wordsworth determines that the poem's climax—the final decay of the cottage and Margaret's decline—was actually the first part of the poem to be completed. The lines "In sickness she remained; and here she died, / Last human tenant of these ruined walls" have an even earlier source in *The Descriptive Sketches* of 1793:

> There be those whose lot far otherwise is cast:
> Sole human tenant of the piny waste,
> By choice or doom a gipsy wanders here,
> A nursling babe her only comforter;
> Lo, where she sits beneath yon shaggy rock,
> A cowering shape half hid in curling smoke!
>
> [173-78]

The image of the deserted woman in an environment of decay and waste is thus the source and impetus of the poem. Beginning with the condition of decay and death, *The Ruined Cottage* is indeed a form of elegy. It mourns the same loss as *Peele Castle* and the *Ode.* That loss is implicit in the very opening of the poem. The poet first describes a clear and pleasant sunny scene. The sunshine, he states, is

> Pleasant to him who on the soft cool moss
> Extends his careless limbs beside the root
> Of some huge oak whose aged branches make
> A twilight of their own, a dewy shade
> Where the wren warbles while the dreaming man,
> Half-conscious of that soothing melody,
> With side-long eye looks out upon the scene,
> By those impending branches made more soft,
> More soft and distant.
>
> [10-18]

The poet begins with this "soft and distant" dreamlike scene of harmony and repose between humanity and Nature only to contrast it with his real present condition:

> Other lot was mine.
> Across a bare wide Common I had toiled
> With languid feet which by the slipp'ry ground
> Were baffled still, and when I stretched myself
> On the brown earth my limbs from very heat
> Could find no rest, . . .
>
> [18-23]

The earth does not, as in the first stanza, soothe and cradle; on the contrary, it is "bare," "brown," and "slippery" and offers the poet no comfort or rest. The subject of *The Ruined Cottage*, as of the *Ode*, is the lost harmony between mother and child, embodied in the ruptured relationship between Nature and humanity. Whereas the *Ode* is a meditative piece, *The Ruined Cottage* dramatizes the poet's confrontation with that loss in the story of Margaret.

Margaret's tale is told by an old pedlar whom the poet first encounters sleeping beneath the elms. Feeling thirsty and oppressed himself, the poet is struck by the old man's peaceful repose. "I guess he had no thought," he remarks, "Of his way-wandering life" (45-46). The poet also happily observes that the man's hat is "Bedewed with water-drops as if the brim / Had newly scooped a running stream" (50-51). The pedlar, sated and at peace with his environment, will serve in the course of the poem as the agent for the poet's reconciliation with Nature. The pedlar will share with the poet his experience of Margaret, and Margaret's story will impress in the heart of the poet, as it has in the pedlar, a deep and reassuring tranquility.

The pedlar's narration of Margaret's history is prefaced by a long descriptive passage. The specific details of the setting reveal the narcissistic wound, the oral deprivation and frustration, at the source of the poem. The pedlar leads the poet through a garden, overgrown and "cheerless," to a well "Half-covered up with willow-flowers and grass." He tells the poet,

> . . . "I see around me here
> Things which you cannot see. We die, my Friend,
> Nor we alone, but that which each man loved
> And prized in his peculiar nook of earth
> Dies with him, or is changed, and very soon
> Even of the good is no memorial left."
>
> [67-72]

Through hearing and sympathizing with Margaret's suffering, the poet will confront this reality of loss, pain, and death. At the same time, however, he will come to understand "the strong creative power / Of human passion" implicit in the tale. That power, the pedlar says, is heard in poets' elegies and songs lamenting the dead. There are, he asserts, "Sympathies . . . / More tranquil, yet perhaps of kindred birth, / That steal upon the meditative mind / And grow with thought" (80-83). Like Wordsworth in the *Ode*, the poet in *The Ruined Cottage* will learn to find the strength "In the soothing thoughts that spring / Out of human suffering." At the moment, however, the poet experiences only feelings of deprivation and abandonment. He looks at the waters of the spring and feels a kindred sadness:

> . . . Beside yon spring I stood,
> And eyed its waters till we seemed to feel
> One sadness, they and I. For them a bond
> Of brotherhood is broken; time has been
> When every day the touch of human hand
> Disturbed their stillness, and they ministered
> To human comfort. When I stooped to drink
> A spider's web hung to the water's edge,

And on the wet and slimy foot-stone lay
The useless fragment of a wooden bowl.
It moved my very heart.

[82-93]

The overgrown and neglected "half-covered up" well and the broken bowl suggest a rupture in the original oral relationship with the mother. Jonathan Wordsworth notes that this passage, and *The Ruined Cottage* as a whole, has its source in the fragment *Incipient Madness*, written around 1795. The traveler in *Incipient Madness* crosses a "dreary moor" and discovers a ruined hut, and "At a small distance, on the dusky ground / A broken pane which glittered in the moon / And seemed akin to life." Like the broken bowl in *The Ruined Cottage*, the broken pane inspires feelings of profound loss and grief:

. . . There is a mood
A settled temper of the heart, when grief,
Become an instinct, fastening on all things
That promise food, doth like a sucking babe
Create it where it is not. From this time
That speck of glass was dearer to my soul
Than was the moon in heaven . . .

[7-13]

In an earlier version, the poet states that the speck of glass "could produce / A feeling of absence" and he waits for the moment when his sight "Should feed on it again." The oral basis of the loss is clear. A similar image occurs in the 1793 version of *An Evening Walk*. Wordsworth describes a sick and weary mother, a soldier's widow, traveling with her children along the road, and he remarks, "For hope's deserted well why wistful look? / Chok'd is the pathway, and the pitcher broke" (255-56).

In the final paragraph of *Incipient Madness*, the poet encounters the woman of the hut with "a pitcher in her hand / Filled from the spring." She turns to him

. . . and in a low and fearful voice
By misery and rumination deep
Tied to dead things, and seeking sympathy
She said: "that wagon does not care for us" —

The words were simple, but her look and voice
Made up their meaning, and bespoke a mind
Which being long neglected, and denied
The common food of hope, was now become
Sick and extravagant . . .

[50-61]

The portrait is a familiar one in Wordsworth's poetry; the woman, abandoned, "neglected and denied," grows mad, "sick and extravagant." Ruth, for instance, was left as a child "half desolate" and "slighted" by the death of her mother. She wanders off into nature and becomes "an infant of the woods." As a young woman, however, she is deserted again, this time by her soldier lover, and "such pains she had, / That she in half a year was mad." Ruth turns back to the woods and lives out her short life "alone, / Under the greenwood tree" (*Ruth*, 1799).

The young mother in *Her Eyes Are Wild* (1798) is also considered mad, and she too suffers from the desertion of her husband. She fears that her child will grow mad as well—"What wicked looks are those I see? Alas! that look so wild, / It never, never came from me: / If thou art mad, my pretty lad, / Then I must be for ever sad." Also turning to the woods for solace, she promises the boy that they will find the father in the woods and "laugh and be gay" and "live for aye." Nature offers no salvation, however, for Martha Ray in *The Thorn*. She has grown so distracted by the desertion of her betrothed that she is rumored to have killed her baby, hung him on a tree, and buried him beneath a hill of moss. The natural landscape in *The Thorn* is desolate and stormy and Martha Ray herself is identified with that landscape; the narrator first mistakes her figure for a "jutting crag."

The infant's experience of loss and betrayal in relation to the mother thus lies at the heart of Wordsworth's image of the deserted woman. The mother is imaged as hostile and treacherous, in the form of a denying and rejecting Nature, and also as a suffering victim, in the figure of the deserted woman. The infant/poet's angry aggressive feelings toward the mother indeed make him feel as if he has betrayed her as well as she him. By suffering and confronting these feelings in the course of the poems, however, the poet emerges from his mourning with renewed faith in the essential goodness and love in the mother, in the self, and, by extension, in humanity.

As the pedlar begins the story of Margaret, the first thing he mentions, as an example of her goodness, is her offering "cool refreshment drawn / From that forsaken spring" to every passing traveler who came her way. Throughout the poem, the cool waters of the spring (associated with Margaret's goodness) are contrasted with a cruel dryness and desolation. "The good die first," the Pedlar asserts, "And they whose hearts are dry as summer dust / Burn to the socket." Margaret's cottage too is now "stripped," "bare," dry, and rotting:

> . . . She is dead,
> The worm is on her cheek, and this poor hut,
> Stripped of its outward garb of houshold flowers,
> Of rose and sweet-briar, offers to the wind
> A cold bare wall whose earthy top is tricked
> With weeds and rank spear-grass. She is dead,
> And nettles rot and adders sun themselves
> Where we have sate together while she nursed
> Her infant at her breast. . . .
>
> [103-11]

Again, the present desolation is contrasted with a past image of drinking and satiation, specifically with the feeding at the breast. The simple, repeated phrase, "she is dead" also enforces the essential elegaic nature of the poem.

The pedlar goes on to describe Margaret's husband, a "Sober and steady" man who worked industriously from morning till night in the garden. As Jonathan Wordsworth observes, the act of gardening in the poem is symbolic of the human side of the bond with Nature. The poem centers on the breakdown of that bond. The pedlar describes how "two blighting seasons" left the fields with "half a harvest" and how "it pleased heaven to add / A worse affliction in the plague of war, / A happy land was stricken to the heart" (134-37). Not only has Nature betrayed humanity with her "blighting" draught, but humanity has betrayed her with the affliction of war. The pedlar stresses Margaret's "chearful hope" in this time of hunger and distress. Her husband, however, was not as strong: "Day by day he drooped, / And he would leave his home" and wander into the town or among the fields. His behavior toward his children became strange and wild:

One while he would speak lightly of his babes
And with a cruel tongue, at other times
He played with them wild freaks of merriment,

. . . .

[179-81]

At this point in the narrative, the Pedlar pauses. The thought of the husband's restless and faithless behavior arouses a like fear within himself. He fears that his own "restless thoughts" are "feeding on disquiet" and "disturb / The calm of Nature" (197-98). *The Ruined Cottage* is permeated with guilty feelings of betrayal. Ultimately, however, Margaret, as a figure of steadfast faith and hope, prevails. Unlike her husband, she remained rooted to the home: even when she wanders off in search of Robert, she always returns. This quality of unwavering faith and endurance accounts for the power of the climactic lines, "In sickness she remained; and here she died, / Last human tenant of these ruined walls." Despite destruction and betrayal, the woman's faith, her love, survives.

Part 2 focuses on Margaret's struggle as her condition becomes increasingly desperate. The pedlar describes a visit to the cottage in early spring, two months after Robert's disappearance. Margaret was grief-stricken, yet the pedlar left her "busy with her garden tools," still full of hope and "tender chearfulness." When the Pedlar returned to the cottage at the end of the summer, however, the weeds were beginning to crowd around the door and windows, and in the garden the bindweed "Had dragged the rose from its sustaining wall / And bent it down to earth" (316-17). The pedlar heard a "solitary infant" crying aloud and he describes the spot as "desolate"—"very desolate, / The longer I remained more desolate" (328-29). The condition of the cottage, and the scene as a whole, again portrays that primal experience of abandonment and desolation. Margaret admitted that she had "changed" and had done "much wrong" to herself and her baby (354). She prayed "that heaven / Will give me patience to endure the things / Which I behold at home" (359-61). Her husband had deserted the home and a wild and sinister Nature was encroaching—the weeds had dragged the rose from the wall and "defaced" the garden, and the truant sheep, using her door as a couching place, had left discoloring "dull red stains" and were gnawing at the roots of a young apple tree. "I fear it will be dead and gone," Margaret said of the tree, "ere Robert come again." With simple dignity, Margaret faced the desolation and futility of her condition, and yet she remained in hope.

The pedlar notes Margaret's remark that "but for her Babe . . . / She had no wish to live—that she must die / Of sorrow" (428-31). Peter Manning, in "Wordsworth, Margaret, and the Pedlar," argues that this situation of the infant preserving the mother's life is central to Wordsworth's poetry. It reflects, he says, the poet's infantile fantasy of rescuing the mother and preventing her death. He agrees with Onorato that the images of the mother in the poetry are usually invested with feelings of personal inadequacy and despair. Manning believes, however, that Wordsworth transforms his feelings of loss and his fantasy of reunion with the mother "into a vision of himself as the solitary man communing with nature" (p. 202). In "The Ruined Cottage," however, I see the consolation for the loss lying less in the character of the pedlar than in the character of Margaret herself. Her baby, after all, dies —"She told me that her little babe was dead, / And she was left alone"—and yet Margaret remains alive, bereft of all comfort or sign of hope, quietly enduring. There is no feeling of personal inadequacy surrounding the image of Margaret—her character demands no assistance; she endures alone.

Finally, in some of the most powerful lines Wordsworth ever wrote, the pedlar describes the final decay of the cottage and Margaret's death.

> "Meanwhile her poor hut
> Sunk to decay; for he was gone, whose hand
> At the first nippings of October frost
> Closed up each chink, and with fresh bands of straw
> Chequered the green-grown thatch. And so she lived
> Through the long winter, reckless and alone,
> Till this reft house, by frost, and thaw, and rain,
> Was sapped; and when she slept, the nightly damps
> Did chill her breast, and in the stormy day
> Her tattered clothes were ruffled by the wind
> Even at the side of her own fire. Yet still
> She loved this wretched spot, nor would for worlds
> Have parted hence; and still that length of road,
> And this rude bench, one torturing hope endeared,
> Fast rooted at her heart. And here, my friend,

In sickness she remained; and here she died,
Last human tenant of these ruined walls."

[477-92]

Margaret was "rooted" to this "wretched spot" by her "torturing hope," by her love. This tale of a woman's sufferings, the Poet says at the end, "seemed to comfort me;" he is comforted by the woman's ability to endure her oppression and by the vitality of her love. He returns to the cottage and traces "That secret spirit of humanity / Which, 'mid the calm oblivious tendencies / Of nature, 'mid her plants, her weeds and flowers, / And silent overgrowings still survived." Despite an indifferent and destructive mother, a good and loving mother still survives. Now even the aggressive weeds and spear-grass, which the poet described at the beginning of the poem as "rank" and sinister, are "By mist and silent raindrops silvered o'er" and convey an "image of tranquility," "calm and still," and "beautiful." Margaret's faith, her love, "still survived" despite desertion and destruction, despite the ruin of the cottage, and this is the poet's consolation. In *The Ruined Cottage* Wordsworth faces his feelings of rage and loss and yet confirms his faith in the mother and her love. Because the mother imago is so deeply tied to the poet's sense of identity, to his feeling of self-love, the confirmation of her love also reaffirms his faith in himself.

Feeling calm and assured, the poet can at last leave the cottage: "I turned away, / And walked along my road in happiness." The poet and the pedlar cast a "farewell look / Upon those silent walls" and retire to a "rustic inn," their "evening resting place." Having mourned and accepted his loss, the poet is ready to reenter the daily world, to resume his common rustic life and to find within it the same evidence of humanity's enduring and creative power, the same faith, which he has discovered through hearing the story of Margaret.

AFTERWORD

The familiar image of the Romantic self, the lost and angry outcast figure (what Praz calls the "Fatal Man"), is born of the ambivalent Romantic Mother. The self in the poetry is continually up against its own rage and destructiveness, a rage directed toward both the mother and itself. The finest Romantic poetry, however, reveals the efforts of that self to overcome its angry, self-destructive attachment to the mother, to give the woman back her wholeness, her separate reality, and thereby to make itself whole. Thus, the organic harmony between humanity and Nature, the integrated relationship between self and environment, and the formation of an autonomous identity, an integrated self, often represent the end achievement of the most successful Romantic poems. The common thread in the best works of the various poets is always the acceptance of suffering—the confrontation with loss, pain, and guilt. With the acceptance of personal suffeing comes a larger sense of shared human suffering. Compassion, the Romantics teach us, is the only way out of a self-destroying narcissism.

Certainly, the Romantic poets are more various than they are alike; the works of each are grounded in highly individual personalities. Considered together, however, their works do reflect a dominant psychological problem of their age. That central problem, furthermore, did not end with the period but has continued to affect the psychic lives and kindle the creative imaginations of modern and contemporary writers. The ambivalent relation between the self and its parental imagos—the divided and unresolved inner condition that the Romantics first began to explore—finds its logical extension in the dissociated, distintegrated condition expressed in so many modern works of art. Behind the fragmented condition that these works display can often be detected the same narcissistic wound, the same intense feelings of loss, betrayal, and rage, the same fixation on idealized images of mother and self, as found, for instance, in Shelley's poetry.

Shelley was indeed an important influence for several modern poets and novelists, particularly Yeats and Conrad. Yeats's idealization of women and his aestheticism both reflect regressive narcissistic fantasies. In Conrad's novels, the women figures are also either idealized, shadowy, and unreal, like Kurtz's Intended, or they are phallic and formidable, like Kurtz's African mistress. Much as Shelley's Poet in *Alastor* dies bewailing his wounded and victimized self, so many of Conrad's characters end their lives crying, like Nostromo, "'I die betrayed—betrayed by—'" But, Conrad adds, "he did not say by whom or by what he was dying betrayed." The characteristic modern themes of betrayal and breakdown deserve to be studied in relation to an unconscious ambivalent attitude toward the mother.

In *The Culture of Narcissism* (1978), Christopher Lasch observes that every age develops its own particular form of pathology, and he suggests that "narcissism holds the key to . . . the moral climate of contemporary society." We would perhaps then do well to look to the Romantics, for they were grappling with our own condition. The best of their poetry not only lends impassioned expression to the deep-rooted conflicts inherent in this condition, but it also gives us a glimpse into the struggle necessary to resolving ambivalence and conflict, to finding a way back to the objects outside the self, to moving out of narcissistic isolation and into mature object relations.

NOTES

INTRODUCTION

1. Ernst Kris, *Psychoanalytic Explorations in Art*, pp. 26-31.
2. This is A. E. Rodway's thesis in *The Romantic Conflict*.

1. SHELLEY

1. Raymond Havens, "Shelley's 'Alastor.'"
2. Some critics have attempted actually to "identify" the unnamed Poet. See Earl Leslie Griggs and Paul Mueschke, "Wordsworth as Prototype of the Poet in Shelley's 'Alastor,'" *PMLA* 49, no. 1 (1934): 229-45, and Joseph Raben, "Coleridge as Prototype of the Poet in Shelley's 'Alastor,'" *Review of English Studies* 17, no. 67 (1966): 278-92.
3. Harold Bloom, *The Visionary Company*, p. 286.
4. Herbert Read, "A Defense of Shelley," in *The True Voice of Feeling*, pp. 212-88.
5. Sigmund Freud, "Two Encyclopedia Articles," p. 133.
6. Harry Guntrip, *Personality Structure and Human Interaction*, p. 194.
7. Harry Guntrip, *Schizoid Phenomena, Object Relations, and the Self*, pp. 19-20.
8. Rene Spitz, *The First Year of Life*, p. 42.
9. Melanie Klein and Joan Riviere, *Love, Hate, and Reparation*, pp. 57-119.
10. W. Winnicott, *The Maturational Processes and the Facilitating Environment*, p. 103.
11. Arnold Modell, *Object Love and Reality*, p. 88.
12. Spitz, *First Year of Life*, p. 42.
13. Eustace Chesser, *Shelley and "Zastrozzi,"* arrives at conclusions about Shelley's personality that are similar to my own. Chesser regards *Zastrozzi* as "dream material" and she concludes from her analysis of it that Shelley "was an introspective schizoid type with arrested sexual development at an undifferentiated

stage, showing itself in elements of narcissism, homosexuality and immature heterosexuality" (p. 32). Her study, however, relies exclusively on Freudian and Jungian terminology and defines Shelley's central conflict as one of repressed homosexuality.

14. For a psychoanalytic study of preoedipal and oedipal patterns in Byron's poetry see Peter J. Manning, *Byron and His Fictions.*

15. Rudolf Storch, "Abstract Idealism in English Romantic Poetry and Painting," pp. 192-93.

16. Melanie Klein, *Envy and Gratitude and Other Works, 1946-63* (New York: Dell, 1957), p. 302.

17. Kohut, *The Analysis of the Self,* p. 116.

18. Otto Kernberg, *Borderline Conditions and Pathological Narcissism,* p. 316.

19. Storch, "Abstract Idealism," p. 208.

20. Bloom, *The Visionary Company,* p. 361.

21. Donald H. Reiman, *Shelley's "Triumph of Life": A Critical Study,* pp. 31-33.

2. KEATS

1. Lionel Trilling, "Poet as Hero," pp. 3-49.

2. Both Aileen Ward, in *John Keats,* and Robert Gittings, in *John Keats,* discuss the mother's hasty remarriage after the father's death, her mysterious disappearance for several years, and her loss of legal control of the children.

3. Arthur Wormhoudt, *The Demon Lover,* pp. 70-88.

4. *The Letters of John Keats, 1814-1821,* vol. 3, pp. 103-4.

5. F. R. Leavis, *Revaluation,* p. 261.

6. Gittings, *John Keats,* also discusses the "ultimate enigma" of Keats's mother. He remarks that Keats's "complete silence about her suggests some shattering knowledge, with which, at various times in his life, he can be seen dimly struggling to come to terms" (p. 30).

7. Harold Bloom, *The Visionary Company,* p. 369; Bruce Miller, "On the Meaning of Keats' 'Endymion.'"

8. John Middleton Murry, *Keats,* pp. 176-81.

9. *Ode on a Grecian Urn* is also informed by the ambivalent maternal attachment and reveals a regressive desire to retreat into a world of ideal self-images and object images. The scene on the urn possesses an erotic "Ecstasy" for Keats precisely because it describes mortals or gods in pursuit. Their love, as he describes in stanza 3, is a "happy love" because it is "still to be enjoyed"; it is happy, that is, because it is yet unrealized. The object of desire is not and can never be attained. Similarly, Keats describes the urn as an "unravish'd bride," beautiful because untouched. The ode expresses a desire to avoid the actual moment of erotic fulfillment because of the inevitable pain of rejection and loss. The ode indeed shuns reality. As F. R. Leavis has pointed out, this ideal pastoral of marble men and women is a "Cold Pastoral" (p. 254).

10. Ward, *John Keats,* p. 92.

11. Ibid., pp. 135-37.

12. Ibid., p. 143.

13. The rage and desolation at the root of the oral experience are evident throughout the *Ode*. While the "bee-mouth sips" Pleasure, for instance, the Pleasure is "Turning to Poison"; the moment of fulfillment dissolves ever into the experience of pain and loss. The *Ode* is about the very pleasure in the pain of submission and rejection.

14. A. E. Rodway, *The Romantic Conflict*, p. 241.

15. Walter Jackson Bate, *John Keats*, p. 596.

16. Leavis, *Revaluation*, p. 272.

17. Ibid., p. 261.

18. Autumn is associated, on the one hand, with a dying season, with "mists and mellow fruitfulness" and "the maturing sun," with the melancholy of aging and inevitable loss. In the second stanza, autumn is personified as passive and feminine: she is "sitting careless on a granary floor," with "hair soft-lifted by the winnowing wind," or "sound asleep, / Drows'd with the fume of poppies," or by a cider press, watching "the last oozing hours by hours." At the same time, however, she is "conspiring" with the male sun in the first stanza "to load and bless" the vines with fruit. The vigorous ripening activity suggests a masculine assertiveness, as in

> To bend with apples the moss'd cottage-trees,
> And fill all fruit with ripeness to the core;
> To swell the gourd, and plump the hazel shells
> With a sweet kernel; to set budding more,
> And still more, later flowers for the bees.

The voice of *To Autumn* is not suppressed by the feminine melancholic; it is not overwhelmed by that sense of loss which the infant self experienced in relation to the mother. Having accepted and resolved that loss, Keats is able to find the same creative and self-affirming identity in autumn as he has found in himself.

3. COLERIDGE

1. G. Wilson Knight, *The Starlit Dome*, pp. 83-84.

2. Roy Basler, *Sex, Symbolism, and Psychology in Literature*, pp. 3-51.

3. Gerald Enscoe, *Eros and the Romantics*, pp. 58-59.

4. Thomas Raysor and Max Schultz, "Coleridge," p. 192.

5. William Walsh, *Coleridge*, p. 49.

6. Eugene Sloane, "Coleridge's 'Kubla Khan.'"

7. David Beres, "A Dream, a Vision, and a Poem."

8. Arthur Wormhoudt, *The Demon Lover*, pp. 19-29.

9. D. W. Harding, "The Theme of the 'Ancient Mariner,'" p. 61.

10. Samuel Taylor Coleridge, *Table Talk*, July 6, 1833, in *The Collected Works of Samuel Taylor Coleridge*.

11. Beverly Fields, *Reality's Dark Dream*,

12. Harding, "'Ancient Mariner,'" p. 56.

13. Wormhoudt, *The Demon Lover*, p. 11; Heinz Kohut, *The Analysis of the Self*, p. 116.

14. As recounted by Newman Ivey White in *Portrait of Shelley*, p. 203.

15. James Gilman, quoted by Humphry House in *Coleridge*, pp. 301-2.

16. Arnold Modell, *Object Love and Reality*, p. 49.

4. WORDSWORTH

1. Two of the more extreme views are expressed by Edward Bostetter in *The Romantic Ventriloquists*, and Geoffrey Hartman in *Wordsworth's Poetry, 1787-1814*. Bostetter claims that even Wordsworth's early belief in the benignancy of nature is self-deception, while Hartman believes that Wordsworth shows nature, from the beginning, as teaching the mind to be free of nature.

2. Fenwick Notes, in *The Prose Works of William Wordsworth*, vol. 3, p. 194.

3. Jonathan Bishop, "Wordsworth and the 'Spots of Time.'"

4. "The Uncanny," in *Sigmund Freud: Collected Papers*, p. 403.

5. Lionel Trilling, "The Immortality Ode," p. 155.

6. Harry Guntrip, *Personality Structure and Human Interaction*, p. 167.

7. Jonathan Wordsworth, *The Music of Humanity*, pp. 33-49.

BIBLIOGRAPHY

PRIMARY SOURCES

Blake: Complete Writings. Edited by Geoffrey Keynes. London: Oxford University Press, 1966.

The Complete Poetical Works of Lord Byron. 2 vols. Edited by Jerome J. McGann. Oxford: Clarendon Press, 1980.

Coleridge: Poetical Works. Edited by Ernest Hartley Coleridge. London: Oxford University Press, 1967.

The Collected Works of Samuel Taylor Coleridge. 16 vols. Vol. 14. Edited by Kathleen Coburn. Princeton: Princeton University Press, 1978.

The Letters of John Keats, 1814-1821. Edited by Hyder Edward Rollins. Cambridge, Mass.: Harvard University Press, 1958.

The Poems of John Keats. Edited by Jack Stillinger. Cambridge, Mass.: Harvard University Press, Belknap Press, 1978.

Shelley: Poetical Works. Edited by Thomas Hutchinson. London: Oxford University Press, 1971.

The Poetical Works of William Wordsworth. 5 vols. Edited by Ernest De Selincourt and Helen Darbishire. Oxford: Clarendon Press, 1940-49.

The Prose Works of William Wordsworth. 3 vols. Edited by Alexander Grosart. 2d ed., 1876; reprint ed., New York: AMS Press, 1967.

Wordsworth, William. *"The Prelude": A Parallel Text.* Edited by J. C. Maxwell. Harmondsworth: Penguin Books, 1972.

PSYCHOANALYTIC SOURCES

Balint, Michael. "Primary Narcissism and Primary Love." *Psychoanalytic Quarterly*, no. 29 (1960), pp. 6-43.

Freud, Sigmund. "Mourning and Melancholia." In *Collected Papers.* 5 vols. Vol. 4. Edited by Ernest Jones. New York: Basic Books, 1959.

―――――. "On Narcissism." In *Collected Papers.* Vol. 4.

————. "Two Encyclopedia Articles." In *Collected Papers*. Vol. 5.

————. "The Uncanny." In *Collected Papers*. Vol. 4.

Guntrip, Harry, *Personality Structure and Human Interaction*. New York: International Universities Press, 1961.

————. *Schizoid Phenomena, Object Relations, and the Self*. New York: International Universities Press, 1969.

Kernberg, Otto. *Borderline Conditions and Pathological Narcissism*. New York: Jason Aronson, 1975.

Klein, Melanie and Riviere, Joan. *Love, Hate, and Reparation*, 2d ed., 1937; reprint ed., New York: W. W. Norton, 1964.

————. *Envy and Gratitude and Other Works*. New York: Dell Press, 1957.

Kohut, Heinz. *The Analysis of the Self*. New York: International Universities Press, 1971.

Kris, Ernst. *Psychoanalytic Explorations in Art*. 2d ed., 1952; reprint ed., New York: Schocken Books, 1964.

Lasch, Christopher. *The Culture of Narcissism*. New York: W. W. Norton, 1978.

Modell, Arnold. *Object Love and Reality*. New York: International Universities Press, 1968.

Spitz, Rene. *The First Year of Life*. New York: International Universities Press, 1965.

Winnicott, D. W. *The Maturational Processes and the Facilitating Environment*. New York: International Universities Press, 1965.

CRITICAL SOURCES

Basler, Roy. *Sex, Symbolism, and Psychology in Literature*. 2d ed., 1948; reprint ed., New York: Octagon Books, 1967.

Bate, Walter Jackson. *John Keats*. Cambridge, Mass.: Harvard University Press, Belknap Press, 1963.

Beres, David. "A Dream, a Vision, and a Poem: A Psychoanalytic Study of the Origins of 'The Rime of the Ancient Mariner,'" *International Journal of Psychoanalysis*, no. 32 (1951), pp. 97-116.

Bishop, Jonathan. "Wordsworth and the 'Spots of Time.'" In *Wordsworth: The Prelude, A Casebook*. Edited by W. J. Harvey and Richard Gravil, pp. 134-54. London: Macmillan Press, 1972.

Bloom, Harold. *The Visionary Company*. Ithaca: Cornell University Press, 1971.

Bostetter, Edward. *The Romantic Ventriloquists*. Seattle: University of Washington Press, 1963.

Chesser, Eustace. *Shelley and Zastrozzi: Self-Revelation of a Neurotic*. London: Gregg Press, and Archive Press, 1965.

Enscoe, Gerald. *Eros and the Romantics: Sexual Love as a Theme in Coleridge, Shelley, and Keats*. Paris: Mouton Press, 1967.

Fields, Beverly. *Reality's Dark Dream: Dejection in Coleridge*. Kent, Ohio: Kent State University Press, 1967.

Gittings, Robert. *John Keats*. Boston: Little, Brown, 1968.

Harding, D. W. "The Theme of the 'Ancient Mariner.'" In *Coleridge: A Collection of Critical Essays*, edited by Kathleen Coburn. Englewood Cliffs: Prentice-Hall, 1967.

Hartman, Geoffrey. *Wordsworth's Poetry: 1787-1814.* New Haven: Yale University Press, 1964.

Havens, Raymond. "Shelley's 'Alastor.'" *PMLA* 15, no. 1 (1930): 1098-1116.

House, Humphrey. *Coleridge.* London: Rupert Hart-Davis, 1967.

Knight, G. Wilson. *The Starlit Dome.* London: Methuen Press, 1959.

Leavis, F. R. *Revaluation.* London: Chatto and Windus, 1936.

Manning, Peter. *Byron and His Fictions.* Detroit: Wayne State University Press, 1978.

_____. "Wordsworth, Margaret, and the Pedlar." *Studies in Romanticism,* no. 15 (Spring 1976), pp. 195-200.

Miller, Bruce, "On the Meaning of Keats' 'Endymion.'" *Keats, Shelley Journal* 14 (Winter 1965): 35-55.

Murry, John Middleton. *Keats.* New York: Minerva Press, 1955.

Onorato, Richard. *The Character of the Poet: Wordsworth in "The Prelude."* Princeton: Princeton University Press, 1971.

Praz, Mario. *The Romantic Agony.* 2d ed., 1933; reprint ed., London: Oxford University Press, 1951.

Radley, Virginia. "'Christabel': Directions Old and New." *Studies in English Literature,* no. 4 (1964), pp. 531-41.

Raysor, Thomas, and Schulz, Max. "Coleridge." In *English Romantic Poets: A Review of Research and Criticism,* edited by Frank Jordan. New York: MLA of America, 1972.

Read, Herbert. *The True Voice of Feeling.* 2d ed., 1947; reprint ed., London: Faber and Faber, 1968.

Reiman, Donald. *Shelley's "Triumph of Life": A Critical Study.* Urbana: University of Illinois Press, 1965.

Rodway, A. E. *The Romantic Conflict.* London: Chatto and Windus, 1963.

Sloane, Eugene. "Coleridge's 'Kubla Khan': The Living Catacombs of the Mind." *American Imago,* no. 29 (1972), pp. 97-123.

Storch, Rudolf. "Abstract Idealism in English Romantic Poetry and Painting." In *Images of Romanticism: Verbal and Visual Affinities,* edited by Karl Kroeber and William Walling. New Haven: Yale University Press, 1978.

Trilling, Lionel. "The Immortality Ode." In *English Romantic Poets: Modern Essays in Criticism,* edited by M. H. Abrams. New York: Oxford University Press, 1975.

_____. "Poet as Hero: Keats in the Letters." *The Opposing Self.* New York: Viking Press, 1955.

Walsh, William. *Coleridge: The Work and the Relevance.* London: Chatto and Windus, 1967.

Ward, Aileen. *John Keats: The Making of a Poet.* New York: Viking Press, 1963.

Ware, J. Garth. "Coleridge's Great Poems Reflecting the Mother Image." *American Imago,* no. 18 (1961), pp. 331-52.

White, Newman Ivey. *Portrait of Shelley.* New York: Alfred Knopf, 1945.

Wordsworth, Jonathan. *The Music of Humanity.* New York: Harper and Row, 1969.

Wormhoudt, Arthur, *The Demon Lover: A Psychoanalytic Approach to Literature.* 2d ed., 1949; reprint ed., Freeport, New York: Books for Libraries Press, 1968.

INDEX

THE JOHNS HOPKINS UNIVERSITY PRESS

The Romantic Mother
Narcissistic Patterns in Romantic Poetry

This book was composed in Palatino text
and display type by David Lorton, from a
design by Cynthia W. Hotvedt.
It was printed on S. D. Warren's 50-lb.
Sebago Eggshell paper and bound in Kivar-5
by Universal Lithographers.